2020 POWERHOUSE EDITION!

HOW TO SELL BOOKS

BY THE TRUCKLOAD ON AMAZON

**LEARN
HOW TO TURN
AMAZON INTO
YOUR 24/7
SALES
MACHINE!**

PENNY C. SANSEVIERI

MORE BOOKS BY PENNY C. SANSEVIERI

Nonfiction

5 Minute Book Marketing for Authors (Amazon Digital 2018, 2019)

52 Ways to Sell More Books (Amazon Digital 2014, 2019)

How to Sell Books by the Truckload on Amazon
(Amazon Digital 2013, 2018, 2019)

50 Ways to Sell a Sleigh-Load of Books: Proven Marketing Strategies to Sell More Books for the Holidays (Amazon Digital 2018)

How to Revise and Re-Release Your Book: Simple and Smart Strategies to Sell More Books (Amazon Digital 2018)

Red Hot Internet Publicity - 4th Edition (Amazon Digital 2016)

How to Get a Truckload of Reviews on Amazon.com (Amazon Digital 2013)

Red Hot Internet Publicity (Createspace 2013)

Powerful Pinterest (Amazon Digital 2012)

Get Published Today (Wheatmark, 2012)

52 Ways to Sell More Books (Wheatmark, 2012)

Red Hot Internet Publicity (Cosimo 2010)

Red Hot Internet Publicity (Morgan James Publishing 2007)

From Book to Bestseller (Morgan James Publishing, 2007)

Get Published Today (Morgan James Publishing, 2007)

From Book to Bestseller (PublishingGold.com, Inc., 2005)

No More Rejections: Get Published Today! (Infinity Publishing, 2002, 2003)

*Get Published! An Author's Guide to the Online
Publishing Revolution* (1st Books, 2001)

Fiction

Candlewood Lake (iUniverse, 2005)

The Cliffhanger (iUniverse, 2000)

To subscribe to our free newsletter, send an e-mail to
subscribe@amarketingexpert.com.

We'd love to hear your feedback.

Here's how to contact us:

Author Marketing Experts, Inc.

10601-G Tierrasanta Blvd, Suite 458

San Diego, CA 92124

www.amarketingexpert.com

CONTENTS

HOW TO SELL BOOKS BY THE TRUCKLOAD ON AMAZON

HOW TO USE THIS BOOK

As of this writing there are approximately 7 million books on the Amazon site, and more being added every day. There are, according to the best estimates, 4,500 books published each day in the US. Yet only 1% of the authors of those books bother to spend any time optimizing their Amazon page.

What does this mean for you? It means that if you just implement one strategy from this book, you're 90% ahead of most of the authors out there vying for reader attention.

The most efficient way to use this book is to read it from start to finish. But if you're in a rush to acquire some particular knowledge (like the newly updated Amazon Ads section), then feel free to jump ahead. If you're new to the idea of keywords, keyword strings, and enhanced Amazon categories, spend some time in the early chapters getting familiar with terminology and how the Amazon algorithm works.

If you're already an Amazon expert and just here to brush up on your knowledge, then feel free to skim the chapter headings, which are divided up in micro-fashion to allow for easy skimming.

I hope you enjoy this book, and I'd love your thoughts on it, either in a review on Amazon or in a direct email to me: penny@amarketingexpert.com

Wishing you huge Amazon success!

UNDERSTANDING AMAZON

It's not an understatement to say that Amazon has changed everything about book publishing and promotion. It seems like every time Amazon introduces something, the competition jumps on the bandwagon, creating similar products or experiences on their sites.

This is a problem, because the Amazon ecosystem is a tremendous game-changer. Much like Google, it can not only help you find the exact right book you've been looking for, but it can also show you things you never knew you needed.

That's the power of the algorithm, and it's also the power of the ads.

To dissect and understand Amazon is like taking Google apart piece by piece. No one person can do that, but we can uncover various algorithms that can help you achieve more visibility for your book.

But this book is not a quick fix. Why? Because when it comes to Amazon, there are no quick fixes. There's no one single solution. But there are several strategies that, when implemented in tandem, help to create the most optimal visibility for your book.

While many experts talk about keyword strings, categories, and pricing, few experts mention this important fact:

Amazon is more a search engine than a store.

In fact, Amazon is literally the "Google" of online buying.

And with this model in mind, I need to tell you right up front that there is no instant anything when it comes to ranking on Amazon. There's a lot of shortcut software out there, and keyword apps, but time and time again I've been reminded that there's nothing like good, old-fashioned hard work to make your Amazon page soar. Much like ranking on Google, people are always searching for shortcuts, but they rarely work.

Understanding Amazon and knowing how to use it to your advantage are vital to keeping those sales up. Amazon is *the* place for book marketing today. All the way back in June of 2014, *SEOMoz*, a popular search engine optimization blog, talked about Amazon and their ranking system. They said, "If you're an author, you don't care about ranking on Google. You want to rank on Amazon."

Everyone in the search engine world knows Amazon ceased being "just a store" several years ago. Now they are the go-to for anything from books and electronics to fashion and pet food.

And here's another twist: Again, back in November 2014, *SEOMoz* reported on Amazon's new travel service, Amazon Travel. Now on the surface this seems fairly benign. I mean, so what, right? Amazon sells everything else, why not travel?

The problem is, this digs right at the heart of Google's business. Think about it. With Amazon Travel, you can get access to the best pricing and possibly the best reviews, which means sites like Yelp and Google's own review systems will start playing second fiddle to Amazon's long-standing and quite extensive review system. And if Amazon Travel is successful, you could go to this one-stop-shop to find everything from a trip to Maui to a contractor for your room addition.

And let's not forget Amazon Music, Amazon grocery stores, and their Echo technology. Think I'm crazy? Ten years ago, no one thought Amazon would sell anything besides books. This company is making serious moves.

It means, essentially, that Amazon is gearing up to play a whole different game, a game that means more and more people will be searching on Amazon for practically everything they need.

And if it isn't already, Google should be worried.

KEYWORD STRING STRATEGIES FOR GREATER VISIBILITY

Returning to the similarity between Amazon's algorithm and Google's, when you want a website to rank on Google, you need a well-chosen set of keyword strings on the homepage, ideally in the copy. It's also smart to have keyword strings in your website address to boost your search visibility.

Though Amazon responds differently, the idea is still the same.

First, let's take a look at the four keys to Amazon ranking:
- Popularity of your title
- Matching search term
- Social proof/reviews
- Pricing strategy

I'll show you how to hit each of these algorithm triggers shortly.

Despite the insane number of books on Amazon, you can still be on page one or claim the number one ranking.

Why? Because most people aren't aware that Amazon is its own search engine. But now you *are* aware, and you can use the information to your advantage. Keep in mind that the tools shared in this book won't guarantee your book hits the number one spot on Amazon, but they will help you generate a significant amount of attention. And in the end, isn't that what you want?

UNDERSTANDING AMAZON METADATA

There was a time when no one talked about metadata. Now it's a buzzword. But metadata means different things, depending on the website where you're planning to sell your book. So it's important to know how Amazon differs. The only things related to metadata that Amazon cares about are your keyword strings and your book's (enhanced) categories.

Zeroing in on Amazon's metadata is a fantastic way to generate more attention for your book, and the great thing is, everything counts. Your book title, subtitle, and keyword strings—all of it matters. Let's take a closer look at metadata, so you can see what I mean.

MAKING YOUR BOOK MORE SEARCHABLE

The more searchable your book is, the more often it's going to come up in searches, and consequently, the more you'll sell. Part of this is due to Amazon's metadata, which is accessible to any author who has their book on Amazon, but most authors and publishers don't use it or understand it.

KDP, Amazon's Kindle Direct Publishing program and Amazon's eBook partner, is a popular way to get your book onto the Amazon platform. But it isn't the only way to populate keyword strings into the Amazon system. If you've published using Ingram/Spark or some other method that allows you to populate keywords into your metadata, these will wind up helping you on the Amazon site as well, because the keywords will get pushed through that system.

For the purposes of this chapter, and to keep it simple, I'm going to focus on the KDP dashboard. Just know that everything you learn here can be applied to virtually any dashboard you publish on. And if you're reading this and you're traditionally published, this will work, too. And later in this book I'll show you how to do this search and hand the results over to your publisher.

If you've published on Amazon via KDP, the screenshot of the dashboard below will probably look familiar to you. This dashboard is where you access all your books' metadata, with the exception of enhanced categories, which I'll discuss in a bit.

3. Target Your Book to Customers

Categories (What's this?)

BUSINESS & ECONOMICS > Marketing > Direct
LANGUAGE ARTS & DISCIPLINES > Authorship

Add Categories

Search keywords (up to 7, optional) (What's this?)

selling books on amazon, how to sell on amazon, make money on amazon, sell books on amazon, sell books online, sell books to amazon, sell books amaz

0 keywords left

You can see you're allowed up to seven search keywords, which should be keyword phrases, or strings. Although Amazon says they're optional, this should *never* be overlooked. While I was doing research for this book, I asked ten authors to let me take a look at the back end, behind-the-scenes details of their books, with the caveat that I wouldn't add terms they didn't need. *None* of them had search words listed. Categories are always a given—all my authors had chosen their categories—but search keywords (and enhanced categories) are often ignored.

We're going to dig into keyword/keyword string strategies in a few chapters, but for now just start percolating some ideas. You've also no doubt seen from the above screenshot that I'm using keyword strings and *not* single keywords. We'll discuss that more in depth, too!

MONITORING KEYWORD STRINGS

Once you've selected your keyword strings, it's important to continually monitor them. And you may not want to stick with the same strings for the duration of your book's life on Amazon.

Why? Because search habits change, some searches are more popular than others, and you won't know which will get you the most bounce until you start playing with a variety of terms. I recommend you start a spreadsheet with the various keywords/keyword strings you've selected for your book and keep track of where your book is ranking whenever you search these terms.

Do not, under any circumstances, use anything other than standard words and phrases for your keyword strings. You can use words and phrases like "romance," "contemporary romance," and even things like, "Kindle deals under $3.99," as long as your book fits that pricing.

But you can no longer use author names and/or book titles. However, as we'll discuss later in this book, you can use names and/or titles with the Amazon Ad System. But for metadata-related keyword strings, it's still against Amazon's Terms of Service.

THINKING IN SEARCH ENGINE TERMS

As you'll learn throughout this book, work you do on Amazon is similar to what I would recommend if you were trying to get traction on Google for your website. This is the mindset you must embrace. Unfortunately, I haven't found discussions of this mindset in many of the books I've read on this topic.

And therein lies yet another problem:

About a year and a half ago, there were dozens of "How to Sell on Amazon" books on the market. Now the number has dwindled to just a few.

Why? I think a lot of it has to do with the fact that Amazon has changed and continues to change all the time. A lot of people thought they had it figured out, then apparently gave up. If you want to stay current with what Amazon is doing, after you've finished reading this book, be sure to subscribe to our blog at www.amarketingexpert.com/blog, where I regularly post updates about changes in Amazon's algorithms and the new programs they launch.

Using a search engine mindset, it becomes clear that in order to get ranking for your website, you need a few things.

1. Metadata: Keyword strings that your market is searching for.
2. An attractive website: Believe me, the days of Google ranking bad-looking sites are over. And by "good-looking," I don't necessar-

ily mean pretty. Just no train wrecks—sloppy-looking sites that were cobbled together with no clear navigation or purpose.

3. Consistent blog posts: Google likes this, because it tells Google the site is being updated frequently, which helps your search results.

Now, if we turn to Amazon, and translate this to book/product speak, we see that similar rules apply:

1. Metadata: Keywords, keywords, keywords—Amazon loves keywords (i.e. keyword strings) and applying that knowledge skillfully will help you achieve better ranking.

2. A good book cover: While Amazon may not ding you for a bad-looking cover, your potential readers most certainly will.

3. Reviews: Consistently getting new reviews is likened to blogging on your website on a regular basis. It shows there's consistent activity. Reviews also help with the visibility of your page and your ranking on Amazon—even if your book is a few years old.

I'll go into each of these in more depth later on in the book!

THE OTHER SIDE OF AMAZON

In addition to the search engine side of Amazon, there is still the store, and, as a retailer, Amazon's goal is to sell stuff, and a lot of it.

We'll talk in more depth about the retailer aspect later on in this book, but one thing I've learned is that most authors list their books on Amazon and think they're done. They just assume Amazon will do the selling for them. This couldn't be further from the truth. There are certain strategies you *must* implement before you can relax a bit.

Aside from being a great place to sell your book, Amazon can become an author's best friend with the application of a little bit of know-how.

In addition to the mysterious search engine component I will unravel for you shortly, there's also the brick-and-mortar type sales model Amazon uses.

Let's say you're the manager of a clothing store, and one day you notice your cashmere sweaters (last season's style) are selling. Normally you wouldn't put them at the front of your store, since you leave that area for the "known hits"—meaning the most trending products, the ones you know will sell well, right? But when something you hadn't expected to sell at all starts gaining interest, you naturally figure it's a good idea to give it more exposure. So you put it a bit closer to the front.

Now the sweaters are selling even faster. So you move them to one of the front tables. Bingo! You sell even more. Then one day, when you're redoing your storefront window, you think: *Let's display them here.* Suddenly your stock is sold out.

This is essentially what happens with Amazon, except replace the sweater with your book. When your book starts selling on Amazon, this superstore takes notice, and your book starts popping up in all sorts of places that relate to book recommendations.

If you own a Kindle, you know when you're looking to buy a book or have just finished reading one, the system shows you other books on the same or similar topics. This is one of the many ways Amazon pushes a book that's selling or showing great promise.

Have you ever wished you could see your book there? How exactly does it happen, and how can you make it work for you?

That's where the algorithm/search engine model and this book come into play. What I'll show you relates to algorithm triggers within Amazon's search function.

Almost 100% of the time, when I look at Amazon author profiles, I find authors aren't doing much to promote their titles. Many of your book promotion tasks require your own "marketing muscle." Much of that marketing muscle is actually marketing know-how—a skill most of us aren't born with.

Regardless of the age of your book, if your subject matter is still relevant, you can boost it on Amazon using these techniques. I've seen it happen with books that are five years old or more. If you're reading this and wondering if you can make it work for your book, let me assure you, you can!

Everything I recommend in this book is free and will only cost you time spent on research and tracking. Some things I show you may have immediate results, as I mentioned earlier in this chapter; others will take a bit of time. Once you implement these strategies, however, it's a bit of "set it and forget it," meaning that once you've done the heavy lifting, the algorithm kicks in and Amazon does the rest.

WHAT PUBLISHING LOOKS LIKE NOW

According to many sources, 4,500 books are published *every day* in the United States, and, while that number is staggering, it's not even close to being accurate.

Why? Because it only includes ISBNs registered in the system. It doesn't count books uploaded straight to Amazon using their internal ASIN number.

Think about this for a minute. How does the staggering number of books published daily affect your title?

Well, for one thing it makes your book harder to find. Therefore, putting intelligent, informed effort into your Amazon page is crucial. But also consider whether having only one book out there is enough to draw attention to yourself and your brand.

In this chapter, we'll look at a few other success strategies you may want to incorporate in your marketing plan.

SHORT IS THE NEW LONG

In most cases, having one book isn't enough to gain traction, because often your first book is your loss leader. It's hard to hear, but it's true—at least in most cases. And while your book may be the exception, I've learned having multiple books out there is a smart idea.

If you find the thought of publishing multiple books discouraging, consider this: The books don't have to be long. This book, for example is actually two books. Each is between 70 and 80 pages each. Not all that long, right?

Short is the new long. I've spoken to a number of fiction authors who've said their 50- to 75-page novellas are doing better than their longer counterparts. Shorter books are selling. Which means you could release one long book a year and then boost sales by publishing a few novellas or shorter, nonfiction how-to guides, manuals, and so on. As long as they're relevant, helpful, and/or entertaining, there's no reason they can't continue to sell, which will help enhance your bookshelf presence on Amazon.

THE AGE OF THE BOOK BUNDLE

Bundling isn't new, but it is hot. But it's not just for fiction. I've done book bundles for my nonfiction books, too. Remember, long books are not going away, but these days, shorter books are having a significant impact on sales. Book bundles are another great way to own the "virtual shelf," or search results page, which also helps with your Amazon visibility.

Consider this: If you have both short and longer books, or a longer book you've serialized—or chopped up into two, three, or four parts—and someone goes searching on Amazon for your topic, wouldn't it be nice to fill the Amazon search page with your book? That's an additional benefit of the book bundle.

I was at a writers' conference recently where an author asked me what he could do with his older, 400-page sci-fi novel. He wanted to re-release it. I suggested he divide the book into four parts, releasing each as a separate book on Amazon, and then bundle them into the full novel.

If you take this route, however, with a series that's tightly connected (meaning a continuation), make sure you have a page at the beginning of each book summarizing the previous book, and at the back of each book to lead the reader to the next book in the series.

Splitting up your books and bundling them will also revive your publication date and bring it current.

It will open up options for promotion and reviews, too.

COMBINING FORCES

I've also noticed authors collaborating on book bundles. In fact, even big-name, best-selling authors are doing it. With the rising popularity of the book bundle, I think we'll see a lot more of this.

I've talked with a few authors who are combining their titles with other authors' titles just so they can keep putting out fresh titles on Amazon. With all the new books out there, it's going to be important for authors with a strong following to support each other by combining books, and perhaps even combining book tours.

In addition to novellas and book bundles, including different authors combining their efforts, I'm seeing more audio books on the market. Offering your books in a variety of formats will be important going forward.

THE SURGE OF AUDIO AND PRINT

While eBooks will continue to be popular, authors who have gone exclusively to eBooks are learning it's important to make their books available in multiple formats in order to stay competitive.

It's never a bad idea to have a book in print. In fact, if you want to succeed in spite of the deluge of new titles published every year, it's wise to have your book in eBook format, print *and* in audio format. Audiobook popularity is growing rapidly, with new titles emerging from this channel all the time, including a lot of indie titles previously available in eBook format only. As indie publishing continues to grow, books available in multiple formats will stand out from those in eBook format only.

We'll address the benefits of print later.

THE BAR IS OFFICIALLY RAISED

It's here—that raised bar we all keep talking about. With the hundreds and thousands of books now published, many (more than ever) will go unnoticed. *Right now the average sale for a self-published book is one hundred copies. Total. Forever.*

I predict that number will drop to ten or less. Shocking? Not really. And fewer than 1% of all books published will ever make it to bookstore shelves. A lot of authors aren't prepared for the marketing or the work it takes to get their book out there. Now more than ever, you'll need not just a good product, but an outstanding one.

One of the reviewers we work with says the biggest reason she turns down a book is because it lacks good editing. Many indie titles suffer from this, unfortunately. The days of shortcuts, self-editing, and self-designed covers are gone. Bring your A-game, or don't play at all.

STREET TEAMS AND SUPERFANS

Now, more than ever before, it's important to engage your fans. A few writing events I spoke at talked about "street teams," but "superfans" is essentially the same concept: Get fans to help you sell books. I mention both here so you'll recognize the terminology when you see and hear it.

Okay, how do you make this strategy work for you? First, you need to make your readership feel important. Make them feel as though they're a critical element in the success of the book, because they are! Offer them exclusive specials and incentives. Remind them often how important they are to you and offer them free "swag" (fun promotional gifts like coffee mugs or bookmarks) to share with their friends (other potential readers).

One of the authors at a Romance Writers of America conference talked about a reader who owns a hair salon. This author sent sample books, bookmarks, and other swag for her friend to put in the shop. It went over so well the salon owner keeps asking for more.

Be creative with your street teams, and if you need help with something, ask them. You'll be surprised how quickly reader/author bonds are formed, and how readers who love your books are willing to go the extra mile.

ADVERTISING IS THE NEW NORMAL

Advertising on sites like Amazon, on social media, and through book-specific platforms like BookBub is quickly becoming a staple for successful authors, who realize it's getting harder and harder to stay in front of potential buyers and new fans in between releases. It's also a relatively self-sustaining strategy once you become adept at analyzing your ad's performance and modifying as you go.

HOW TO RESEARCH KEYWORD STRINGS

When you built your website, your web designer most likely asked you about keywords. Most of you had no idea what keywords were unless you had someone helping you, and odds are you gave your designer a blank stare. Maybe you offered them a few keywords you thought might help, but in all likelihood the ones you came up with weren't very helpful.

When we talk about keywords, it's very important to think in terms of keyword *strings*, because that's how people search. Consider the last search you did on Google. Did you hop over to the search engine and pop in one keyword like *mystery* or *romance*? Likely not. You probably plugged in a string of keywords like, "most romantic weekend getaways," or, "best mystery dinner theatres." Whether you're talking about Google or Amazon searches, they both respond better to keyword strings than to single keywords.

Just about everything we'll talk about ties back to your keyword strings, which is why I decided to include this in-depth discussion that unravels the often-mysterious concept. You'll likely refer to this chapter often, since various places in the book will tie back to it.

Finally, the keyword strings we're looking at will all fall under a basic economic principle: supply and demand. Meaning what we're aiming for is very little supply for something that's in high demand.

This chapter will show you exactly how to do that.

Amazon Tip!

You're allowed up to seven keyword strings when you upload your book to Amazon's Kindle Direct Publishing (KDP). I suggest you come up with a minimum of fifteen keyword strings while you're doing research, so you can swap them out and/or use them in your book description, product page blurbs, enhanced book description, review pitches, and so on.

GETTING STARTED

When you're starting out, finding keyword strings can seem like an arduous and complex task, but it doesn't have to be. I'll show you a few simple ways to build your keyword strings on Amazon. First, you'll need some time. I'd start by carving out an hour or so to start building your list.

WHAT ABOUT USING SOFTWARE?

Generally I'm opposed to keyword software because I always find that the searches on Amazon tend to be more accurate. However, I have used the *Google Adword Planner*, as I'll discuss in a bit, as well as *Keywords Everywhere*, which I'll share with you as well.

But the best kinds of keyword strings are ones you found manually. Why? Because with so many books being published on Amazon, it would be hard for any software—even Google's robust *Keyword Planner*—to give you 100% accurate results.

BUILDING IDEAS

It always helps if you know the keywords and keyword strings your audience tends to use. If you don't know—and this often happens with nonfiction authors, you'll want to start by testing some keyword strings to find out what seems to work well for your book, subject matter, niche, or genre.

SEARCHING FOR GREAT KEYWORD STRINGS ON AMAZON

First, if you're doing a search on Amazon to find keyword strings for your Kindle Direct Publishing dashboard and individual books, I suggest by starting on the Kindle side of the Amazon website.

Not every search is created equal, and searching for "mystery and suspense" on the main Amazon site instead of digging down into the Kindle department specifically, will net you very different and largely inaccurate results.

Also, since so many books are eBooks only, that side of Amazon is denser than their print book side and yields a better representation of what you're really competing against.

To begin your keyword string search, first select Kindle Store from the dropdown (left-hand side of the search below), leaving the search bar blank, and click the orange search button (with the magnifying glass symbol).

Next, click "Kindle eBooks."

Show results for

Kindle Unlimited

☐ Kindle Unlimited
  Eligible (1,515,304)

Prime Reading

☐ Prime Reading Eligible (737)

Audible Narration

☐ eBooks with Audible
  Narration (97,573)

New Releases

Last 30 days (100,345)
Last 90 days (257,173)
Coming Soon (17,094)

Kindle Store

Amazon Device
Accessories (2,242)
Amazon Devices (407)
Kindle Blogs (16,026)
Kindle Newsstand (2,063)
Kindle Newspapers (156)
Kindle Short Reads (1,276,347)
Kindle Singles (1,320)
Kindle Worlds (2,171)
Kindle eBooks (5,094,303)

Once you're there, just start typing your keywords into the search bar. While you're keying them in, Amazon's intuitive search will start to drop down suggestions. Not all of the suggestions will be ones you'll use, but they're certainly a good start.

Ideally you want your keyword string to match the following criteria:

- Make sure you're only using keyword strings. Do not settle for single keywords, because consumers don't search that way. You wouldn't Google with just the word "suspense," either.
- Don't assume Amazon's recommendations, such as those from the above screenshot, are the exact right ones for your book. We'll look at how to determine that in a minute.
- Once you've collected Amazon's suggestions, you'll want to pop over to those pages and see what kinds of books are listed on the results page, AND what their sales rank is. Because if you're using a keyword string with a very high sales rank, it means not many people are actually using that particular keyword string. We'll discuss this more later in this book.
- Be sure to check and see if there are a number of free books cluttering the first page of a particular keyword string search. Let's say you're looking at, "Suspense mystery books." You notice lots of books on free promotion, which will always be at the top of the list. Don't bother to look at their sales rank, because it's not an accurate depiction of how this string is actually doing. Instead, keep going down the list until you find a book that isn't on a pricing promo.
- Don't worry if the search string includes books in Kindle Unlimited. It won't affect your results.

TAKING IT STEP-BY-STEP

Now let's break this down even further. Let's say you have a book that teaches folks how to create a home office, or build a business from home, and so on. The keyword string I'd start with would be: *working from home*. And you'll note from the screenshot below that the number of books in that particular search term is only 1,000. Which means a relatively low supply. Considering that there are 7 million books on Amazon (and growing daily), 1,000 books is a reasonably low number. So in terms of "supply" we're in a good place. Next up we're going to check the demand for this keyword string.

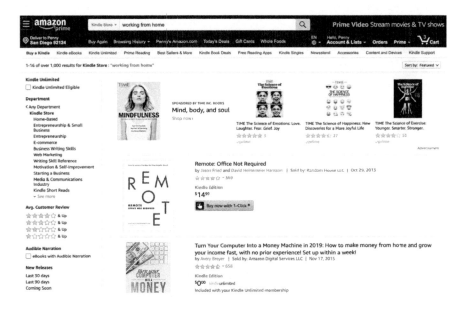

It's important to note here that the search that's popped up is a list of books that are somewhat older, which does not impact the integrity of the keyword string. Next I'm going to click on the first three books to check their sales ranks. Note: none of the books at the top of this string were new, but their sales ranks were all pretty impressive.

About the Author

JASON FRIED and DAVID HEINEMEIER HANSSON are the founders of 37signals, a trailblazing software. They're also contributors to *Signals v. Noise*, one the of Web's most popular blogs.

See all Editorial Reviews

Product details

File Size: 9030 KB
Print Length: 258 pages
Publisher: Currency (October 29, 2013)
Publication Date: October 29, 2013
Sold by: Random House LLC
Language: English
ASIN: B00C0ALZ0W
Text-to-Speech: Enabled
X-Ray: Enabled
Word Wise: Enabled
Lending: Not Enabled
Screen Reader: Supported
Enhanced Typesetting: Enabled
Amazon Best Sellers Rank: #55,521 Paid in Kindle Store (See Top 100 Paid in Kindle Store)
      #8 in Office Management (Kindle Store)
      #14 in Office Management (Books)
      #14 in Human Resources & Personnel

Would you like to **tell us about a lower price?**

Product details

File Size: 503 KB
Print Length: 81 pages
Simultaneous Device Usage: Unlimited
Publisher: Impeccable Publishing (November 17, 2015)
Publication Date: November 17, 2015
Sold by: Amazon Digital Services LLC
Language: English
ASIN: B0185Z29LY
Text-to-Speech: Enabled
X-Ray: Enabled
Word Wise: Enabled
Lending: Enabled
Screen Reader: Supported
Enhanced Typesetting: Enabled
Amazon Best Sellers Rank: #14,985 Paid in Kindle Store (See Top 100 Paid in Kindle Store)
> #2 in Media & Communications Industry (Kindle Store)
> #7 in Business Writing Skills (Kindle Store)
> #8 in Web Marketing (Kindle Store)

Would you like to **tell us about a lower price?**

Related Video Shorts | Upload your video

Product details

File Size: 3338 KB
Print Length: 239 pages
Simultaneous Device Usage: Unlimited
Publisher: Rainmaker Press (March 30, 2016)
Publication Date: March 30, 2016
Sold by: Amazon Digital Services LLC
Language: English
ASIN: B01CTMI7R4
Text-to-Speech: Enabled
X-Ray: Enabled
Word Wise: Enabled
Lending: Enabled
Screen Reader: Supported
Enhanced Typesetting: Enabled
Amazon Best Sellers Rank: #38,850 Paid in Kindle Store (See Top 100 Paid in Kindle Store)
> #16 in Job Hunting (Kindle Store)
> #25 in Starting a Business
> #33 in Home-Based Small Businesses

Would you like to **tell us about a lower price?**

These sales ranks are all pretty good, especially for older books. Which means we now have a keyword string that exactly meets the right criteria: low supply, high demand. And you'll want to do this several more times until you have all the keyword strings you'll need.

Sales rank indicates a book's sales in relation to other books' sales. A book ranked number 1 has sold the most. So, a high number on the sales rank line isn't good. A book ranking of 88,453 means that 88,452 books are selling better than it is. A great high-sales rank is normally 10,000 or less.

But this also depends to some degree on the genre, niche, or subject matter. For example, a sales rank of 13,000 may not seem great. But for some of my own nonfiction stuff it means they're selling pretty well. In some cases, I'm doing $500-plus in book sales per month at that sales rank. However, when I look at that 13,000 rank in fiction, the sales are often lower.

Anything you've heard about how sales rank works should be taken with a grain of salt, because the numbers can vary depending on the category (genre, niche, or subject matter).

Now let's dig into another example. Let's say you have a royal romance book, so you go onto Amazon and type in, "royal romance." The keyword string shows a relatively low number of books, considering the popularity of the genre:

1-16 of over 6,000 results for Kindle Store : "royal romance"

While 6,000 may seem high, consider how busy the genre is. Romance of any kind is a heavily populated category, so I'm going to go with this term for now and check the sales rank of the titles. When I do, I'm pleasantly surprised. Have a look:

Product details

File Size: 440 KB
Print Length: 324 pages
Page Numbers Source ISBN: 1530212766
Simultaneous Device Usage: Unlimited
Publication Date: February 21, 2016
Sold by: Amazon Digital Services LLC
Language: English
ASIN: B01C3HDE4Q
Text-to-Speech: Enabled ⌄
X-Ray: Enabled ⌄
Word Wise: Enabled
Lending: Enabled
Screen Reader: Supported ⌄
Enhanced Typesetting: Enabled ⌄
Amazon Best Sellers Rank: #10,214 Paid in Kindle Store (See Top 100 Paid in Kindle Store)
    #181 in Women's Psychological Fiction
    #433 in Women's New Adult & College Fiction
    #582 in Contemporary Romance Fiction

Product details

File Size: 2826 KB
Print Length: 243 pages
Simultaneous Device Usage: Unlimited
Publication Date: April 1, 2019
Sold by: Amazon Digital Services LLC
Language: English
ASIN: B07Q5B1J52
Text-to-Speech: Enabled ⌄
X-Ray: Not Enabled ⌄
Word Wise: Enabled
Lending: Enabled
Screen Reader: Supported ⌄
Enhanced Typesetting: Enabled ⌄
Amazon Best Sellers Rank: #1,588 Paid in Kindle Store (See Top 100 Paid in Kindle Store)
      #33 in Holiday Romance (Books)
      #34 in Holiday Romance (Kindle Store)
      #119 in Romantic Suspense (Books)

Would you like to **tell us about a lower price?**

Both of these books have low sales ranks, so I'm definitely going to grab that keyword string and give it a shot.

Side note: You might notice that below the Amazon Best Seller Rank are various numbers like #181 in Women's Psychological Fiction. Ignore those for now. That's Amazon's organic ranking i.e. where readers are finding that particular title. When these aren't aligned with the book itself, it often means that the author or publisher hasn't done the Amazon Optimization work.

FINDING KEYWORD STRINGS WITH THE HIGHEST SEARCHES

As you start searching for keywords, it's important to know that, beyond being a popular search term on Amazon, the ideal keyword string also leads you to books that are selling well, called a "funnel." Surprisingly, not all keyword strings, even those that rank high on Amazon, are terrific funnels. Why? Because although they may be searched frequently, they might not have the types of books your consumer wants.

A lot of times this happens when books are populated to a particular category that doesn't have heavy traffic. The suggestions that pop up on Amazon are suggestions based on frequent *searches*, not sales. Suggested search strings don't necessarily mean they have a high enough frequency of search or enough buyers looking at that category to boost your book sales. It simply means the string is being searched often enough to be noticed and included by an algorithm.

Let's look at how you can determine if a keyword string is right or wrong for your book.

First you need to check out the sales rank of the top books that show up in the keyword string search. For example:

The general rule about supply and demand comes with a few exceptions. First off, you may find a keyword string with a small number of books in it, but checking the sales rank makes you second-guess your options, because the sales rank is very high (meaning the book in question isn't selling a lot of copies). This can happen with some keyword strings. Some may have a small number of books, but the sales rank on the books is pretty high, generally in the one hundred thousands. This means that, yes, there are a small number of books under that search term. But it also means they aren't selling.

The flip side of this is when you think, "Okay, I'll put my book in there and get to the number one spot with little or no effort."

I thought that too, and I shifted a romance book into a narrow keyword string. The book fell like a rock in the rankings, which points us back to this important thing to keep in mind: even if Amazon suggests the keyword string, you still need to do your homework to make sure it's the right choice for you.

Quick side note:

On another example search of "romance and military," the first few titles aren't great with regard to sales rank. Take a look at the covers. They aren't stellar, either. In most cases they could have been better. Why did these titles rank so high if the covers aren't great? I'm betting they tinkered with the keyword strings in the titles. As you'll see, the book titles and subtitles have a lot of extra words added. Have another look at that screenshot.

But don't discount a good cover. In most cases, your cover greatly contributes to whether someone clicks on your book to find out more, or not. Farther down the list, in the next screenshot, you can see the *SEALs of Winter* superbundle, plus screenshots below that of a portion of the super-bundle's product/sales page, and its sales rank.

Buy a Kindle   Kindle eBooks   Advanced Search   Daily Deals   Free Reading Apps   Kindle Singles   Newsstand   Accessories   Kindle Unlimited   Discussions   Manage Your Content and Devices   Kindle Support

Start reading *SEALs of Winter: A military romance superbundle* on the free Kindle Reading App or on your Kindle in under a minute. Don't have a Kindle? Get your Kindle here.

Look Inside ↓

SEALs of Winter: A military romance superbundle [Kindle Edition]

Cora Seton (Author), Elle Kennedy (Author), Zoe York (Author), Anne Marsh (Author), Elle James (Author), Jennifer Lowery (Author), S.M. Butler (Author), Delilah Devlin (Author), Kimberly Troutte (Author), Zoe Jack (Author)

★★★★★ ✓ 108 customer reviews

Kindle Price: **$0.99**

- Length: 926 pages (estimated) ⓘ
- Don't have a Kindle? Get your Kindle here.

Free Kindle Reading App
Anybody can read Kindle books—even without a Kindle device—with the FREE Kindle app for smartphones, tablets and computers.

To get the free app, enter your email address or mobile phone number.

[Enter your email or mobile phone number]   [Send me the link]

Best Books of 2014:
Looking for something great to read? Browse our editors' picks for 2014's Best Books of the Year in fiction, nonfiction, mysteries, children's books, and much more.

Product Details

File Size: 1229 KB

Print Length: 926 pages

Simultaneous Device Usage: Unlimited

Publisher: SOS Ladies (November 18, 2014)

Sold by: Amazon Digital Services, Inc.

Language: English

ASIN: B00OQOO9H0

Text-to-Speech: Enabled ☑

X-Ray: Not Enabled ☑

Word Wise: Not Enabled

Lending: Enabled

Amazon Best Sellers Rank: #246 Paid in Kindle Store (See Top 100 Paid in Kindle Store)
  #9 in Books > Romance > **Military**
  #9 in Kindle Store > Kindle eBooks > Romance > **Military**
  #9 in Kindle Store > Kindle eBooks > Romance > Mystery & Suspense > **Suspense**

Would you like to **give feedback on images** or **tell us about a lower price**? .

SEALs of Winter: A military romance superbundle Nov 18, 2014 | Kindle eBook
by Cora Seton and Elle Kennedy

Kindle Edition
$0.99

[Buy now with 1-Click ®]

Auto-delivered wirelessly

★★★★★ ˅ 108
Sold by: Amazon Digital Services, Inc.

Stay the Night: A Navy Seal Erotic Romance (Take a Chance Book 4) Dec 15, 2014 | Kindle eBook
by Caridad Pineiro

Kindle Edition
$0.99
Available for Pre-order. This item will be released on December 15, 2014.

Book 4 of 4 in the Take a Chance Series

Contract with a SEAL (Special Ops: Homefront Book 3) Oct 23, 2014 | Kindle eBook
by Kate Aster

Kindle Edition
$0.00 kindleunlimited
Subscribers read for free. Learn more.
$2.99 to buy

[Buy now with 1-Click ®]

Auto-delivered wirelessly

★★★★★ ˅ 90
Borrow for free from your Kindle device. Join Amazon Prime
Sold by: Amazon Digital Services, Inc.

Deadly Fallout (Red Stone Security Series Book 10) Dec 9, 2014 | Kindle eBook
by Katie Reus

$7.99 Print Price
Kindle Edition
$2.99
You Save: $5.00 (63%)

[Buy now with 1-Click ®]

Auto-delivered wirelessly

★★★★★ ˅ 27
Sold by: Amazon Digital Services, Inc.

Dangerous Secrets: Callaghan Brothers, Book 1 Nov 19, 2014 | Kindle eBook
by Abbie Zanders

Kindle Edition
$0.00 kindleunlimited
Subscribers read for free. Learn more.
$2.99 to buy

[Buy now with 1-Click ®]

Auto-delivered wirelessly

★★★★★ ˅ 8
Borrow for free from your Kindle device. Join Amazon Prime
Sold by: Amazon Digital Services, Inc.

Worth the Fall (The McKinney Brothers, Book 1) Sep 9, 2014 | Kindle eBook
by Claudia Connor

Despite the fact that the first few books have sagging sales ranks, the fourth book down on the list is doing extremely well, as are all the books that follow it. When you see books at the top of a search string with less than stellar sales ranks, it's likely because they just came off of a promotional boost of some kind. If you track these books over time, you'll see their sales ranks quickly plummet as the effects of the promotion wear off.

MORE UNIQUE WAYS TO SEARCH

If you've tried to find something on Google, you have most likely used a search string that involves the word, "and." For example, you entered, "Mystery and book," or something along those lines. The same type of search string works on Amazon, but there's a bit of a twist to it. Let me show you what I mean.

Let's say you wrote a romance novel, and you're trying to find out what your potential readers are searching for. Head on over to Amazon and type in, "Romance and," and see what pops up:

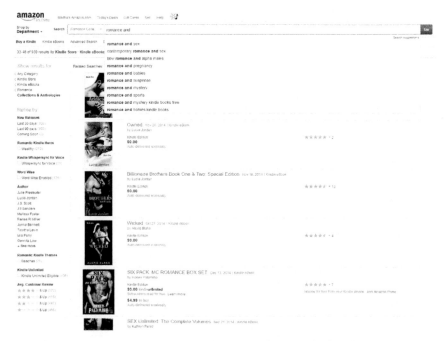

These are autosuggestions based on your keyword plus the word, "and." Now let's take this a step further. Let's add the beginnings of another letter to this, creating a search string that looks like this: "Romance and c." Take a look at the screenshot below:

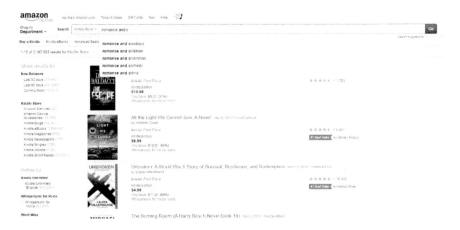

You can see that it brings up even more search suggestions—see the search string "Romance and Christmas?" Fiction authors, particularly romantic fiction authors, take a page from the Hallmark Channel and make sure to incorporate the search term "Romance and Christmas" if their book is set around the holidays. All you have to do is flip through the TV listings to see that, starting at Thanksgiving, Hallmark goes all romance-and-Christmas all the time. It's big business for them, and it should be for you too.

Although it doesn't typically happen in nonfiction, it's still a good idea to remember there are certain keyword strings that change seasonally. Seasonal tie-ins to your topic should be factored into the keyword string only as long as that string is getting enough searches, which we'll cover in the next chapter.

Now you know a little about the different ways to search for optimal keyword strings. Depending on your subject, genre, or niche, you may want to try them all. But remember, if you decide to change your keyword strings, be sure to add them to your book description, and maybe even incorporate them in your title if your book's not "on the shelves" yet.

Also be sure people are actually buying the books in the search results using the keyword strings you're considering. Check the sales rank to be sure it's not too high.

And now you've learned the tools for searching keyword strings and how to use them. You can make use of your knowledge on many levels while you get ready to publish a book that will sell.

AMAZON'S SEARCH FUNCTION

As I showed you in this chapter, Amazon's search function will drop down suggestions much like Google does. But there's a right way and a wrong way to use it.

Take a look at the screenshot below. I typed in, "selling books," and Amazon's top suggestions for this particular keyword string are:

This is where things start to get interesting, because these search suggestions from Amazon will show you what's trending with their consumers. And if you click on one of the search terms, like, "selling books on Amazon," it will take you to the page below, where you'll see another technique for increasing visibility: Several of these authors have included the popular search term in their title, which also helps with their ranking. We'll discuss this more later, too.

If you've already published your book (and likely most of you reading this are in this category), don't worry. There are a lot of other things you can do to help spike your book sales that don't involve changing the title, at least on the cover. Subtitles with keyword strings *can* be added to product pages, though.

But if you haven't put a name on your book yet, you may want to seriously consider using this method to find and use some hot, trending Amazon keywords or keyword strings to include in your title!

CREATING BEST-SELLING BOOK IDEAS

It's one thing to write a book; it's quite another to write a book that will sell. We all want to follow our passion, write our dream, and dance creatively with our muse.

But wouldn't it be fantastic if, amidst all this creativity, we also manage to produce a best-selling book? That is, after all, the dream. This chapter discusses several things you can do to ensure your book targets the largest audience possible.

FINDING BEST-SELLING BOOK IDEAS

I know a gal who's keyed-in to a bunch of SEO people. For those of you not familiar with the term, SEO stands for search engine optimization. These are the folks who spend their lives trying to get on the first page of Google.

Several years back, she and I were talking about how to create ideas that sell. She told me many of her SEO buddies literally write books based only on keywords and keyword strings. It has nothing to do with their passion or even what they want to write about. They focus on saleable terms, meaning phrases getting a huge bounce on Google. This may not be how you'd normally think about writing a book, but there are merits to this methodology. Here are a few things to think about while you plan what to write about:

- **Book focus:** Where will you focus your book? What subject or theme do you want to write about? Don't get too caught up in a set plan. Leave some room for flexibility, but do consider what's hot right now. Your original idea may have been the starting point, but, depending on how long you've been sitting on it, there's a solid chance you can update it a bit to ensure you're responding to current market needs, or to make yourself stand out from competitive titles that hit the market before you.

- **Book title:** As mentioned previously, this is a great place to use keyword strings, so keep an open mind about reworking your title as it gets closer to your publication date. This is also a great time for some market research, because not only should your title include hot keyword strings, it should answer a question or the pique the interest of your potential buyers, and you're often too close to your own work to be aware of hot, trending possibilities…unless you do your due diligence market research.

- **Book subtitle:** If you already have your title, consider using keyword strings in your subtitle to help boost your exposure in searches. And consider whether you want to put your subtitle on your book cover. Leaving it off makes it a lot easier to change it on Amazon to match market needs and industry and genre trends.

- **Book topic:** Let's say you're an expert in your field but aren't sure what topic to write about. Let's say you're a consumer finance guru and want to write a book on this topic. Knowing what consumers are searching for in the area of finance, and what keyword strings are used most often, is a great way to home in on the immediate needs of your readers. Create a topic that's narrower. Instead of addressing a broad area, tighten your focus. It will net you better sales. Consumers like specialized topics that help solve specific problems. And the books don't have to be long. Once you find your market or niche, you'll want to publish regularly for your target audience.

Now, let's assume you've done the keyword string research suggested in this book. Let's see how these searches relate to popular topics on Amazon.

Give this a try:

1. On the Amazon page, search the Kindle store tab. Isolate your searches there for now.

2. Plug in your search term and see what comes up. You'll generally get

five to ten suggestions. Click on one of them.

3. Look at the books that come up in the search and click on the "Customers Also Bought" section.

4. Focus on books with a low sales rank. Depending on the category, it could be as low as 20,000 or as high as 50,000.

5. Make sure there are a variety of books in the Also Bought section, preferably more than five around the same topic, and make sure that they all have this range of sales volume. If it's lower than 20,000, that's great, but neither the super-saturated nor the unpopular categories will help you.

Some Amazon experts say a 20,000 rank indicates the book is selling five copies a day, but I find this hard to prove either way. Just know that, given Amazon's volume, a book is definitely not languishing at that rank.

In addition to topic research, while you're developing your book idea and trying to decide what to include and exclude, consider spending a bit of time comparing the content of other, similar books in your market. Take advantage of Amazon's "look inside" book feature and read several pages, as well as the reviews. Readers will tell you what they want, and they'll often do it in a review. The negative reviews with constructive feedback—those that explain what readers thought was missing or things they wished had been expanded upon—will be especially helpful.

STAYING ON THE SHORT AND NARROW

While full-length books will never go away, there's a trend toward shorter, niche books—books that "own" a narrow market segment. This is also a smart strategy for stretching your knowledge across multiple products, because remember, rarely will one title help you reach your author or business goals.

When I first published *How to Sell Books by the Truckload on Amazon*, I was surprised at how its sales outpaced my other books. While I know the title had a lot to do with this, the book was also shorter and tightly focused on one particular area.

Keep in mind that if you do short, you don't have room for fluff. You'll want to be crystal clear and feature specific instructions, maybe even including step-by-step instructions or checklists, which readers love.

How short can short be? 10,000 to 17,000 words is generally acceptable. Anything under 50 pages is too short; 65 pages is a safe bet, but be cautious when you format your final contents. If your book has too few pages, Amazon's "look inside" feature will reveal most of the content, or enough that readers may glean what they want and not buy it. This is where a thorough (and often longer and more detailed) table of contents comes in very handy, meaning that it creates a good snapshot of what's inside your book—without giving away the store.

If you've finished the book and it still seems a bit too short, consider adding things like checklists, free resources, or bonus chapters from other books you've written that relate to the topic. Of course, don't plump up your page count just to plump it up. Make sure you're adding helpful, useful, relevant information. If the book is too much like a white paper instead of a book, you may end up with a lot of window-shoppers who don't end up buying. And while short is the new long, if you do decide to write shorter books, don't be exclusive about it. Mixing it up is the best route to success.

SIMPLE KEYWORD STRING SUCCESS STRATEGIES TO ROCK YOUR BOOK

Now you understand where your keyword strings come into play in the context of your Amazon back end, behind-the-scenes information, let's take a look at the other ways you can use them.

TITLES AND SUBTITLES

The title of your book can often make or break its success, but most authors haven't considered adding keywords strings to their title and/or subtitle. Many times, particularly in nonfiction, I see authors give their books nebulous titles. This is a mistake, especially when you consider all the titles on Amazon and all the books your reader has to choose from. If you've written nonfiction, be as benefit-driven and as specific as you can be.

But whether or not you've already published your book, there are some key strategies pertaining to subtitles that can really benefit you. Keep in mind that while these examples are for fiction, I chose fiction intentionally. Fiction tends to be a tougher market to use keyword strings in the subtitle, and certainly in the title. But take a look at what some fiction authors are doing, and I'm sure it'll spark some great ideas, regardless of your genre.

SUBTITLES ON FICTION BOOK COVERS

You've probably seen book covers for fiction novels with descriptive subtitles on them before. Take a look at these:

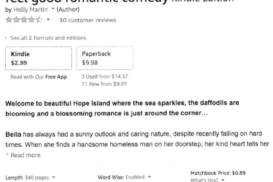

Spring at Blueberry Bay: An utterly perfect feel good romantic comedy Kindle Edition
by Holly Martin ▾ (Author)
★★★★☆ ▾   30 customer reviews

▸ See all 2 formats and editions

Kindle	Paperback
$2.99	**$9.98**
Read with Our **Free App**	3 Used from $14.57
	11 New from $9.97

Welcome to beautiful Hope Island where the sea sparkles, the daffodils are blooming and a blossoming romance is just around the corner...

Bella has always had a sunny outlook and caring nature, despite recently falling on hard times. When she finds a handsome homeless man on her doorstep, her kind heart tells her
▾ Read more

Length: 340 pages ▾   Word Wise: Enabled ▾   Matchbook Price: $0.99
What's this? ▾

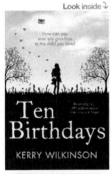

Ten Birthdays: An emotional, uplifting book about love, loss and hope Kindle Edition
by Kerry Wilkinson ▾ (Author)
★★★★☆ ▾   11 customer reviews

▸ See all 2 formats and editions

Kindle	Paperback
$0.99	**$7.99**
Read with Our **Free App**	1 Used from $17.63
	5 New from $7.99

There are going to be so many things I wish I could've told you in person, Poppy. I won't get the chance to do that, so perhaps this is my only way...

It's Poppy Kinsey's birthday.

▾ Read more

Length: 228 pages ▾   Word Wise: Enabled ▾

Two Sisters: A gripping psychological thriller with a shocking twist Kindle Edition
by Kerry Wilkinson ▾ (Author)

▸ See all formats and editions

Kindle
$2.99
Read with Our **Free App**

They told us he had been missing for nearly two days, that he probably drowned. They told us a lie.

Megan was ten years old when her older brother, **Zac**, went missing among the cliffs, caves and beaches that surround the small seaside town of Whitecliff.
▾ Read more

Word Wise: Enabled ▾   Matchbook Price: $6.39 What's this? ▾

New York Times best sellers
Browse the New York Times best sellers in popular categories like Fiction, Nonfiction, Picture Books and more. See more

Here's an example of a great subtitle that isn't listed on the book's cover.

Books › Mystery, Thriller & Suspense › Thrillers & Suspense

Look inside ↓

Those Who Lie: the gripping new thriller you won't be able to stop talking about
Kindle Edition
by Diane Jeffrey ▾ (Author)
⭐⭐⭐⭐☆ ▾   44 customer reviews

› See all formats and editions

Kindle
$0.99

Read with Our **Free App**

'[A] **scorchingly good thriller**' – Lisa Hall, bestselling author of mega-hit *Between You and Me*

'A tantalising and taut thriller with more twists and turns than a corkscrew. Red herrings swim all the way through it. **An excellent page turner**' – Sally (Goodreads)

› Read more

Length: 233 pages ▾   Word Wise: Enabled ▾   Enhanced Typesetting: Enabled ▾

These subtitles give the books a very effective descriptive boost. Readers no longer spend a lot of time reading book descriptions, and vague, "guess what this book is about" book titles just don't work anymore. Now the majority of browsing time is spent with the cover image, title, and subtitle. And you can see how each subtitle above helps further enhance the page while also speaking to the reader's particular goal in finding the right book.

Adding a subtitle on the cover is fine, but keep in mind that if you're sitting in a genre where reader preferences and keyword strings change frequently, you may want to avoid doing that. An example of this might be in the romance genre, where trends tend to change frequently. Sweet romance is a big thing right now, with readers preferring more sweet and less sex. Mentioning it in your subtitle could help increase your sales. Back when *Fifty Shades of Grey* was hitting every bestseller list, sweet/clean romances weren't trending the way they are now. It's important to remain aware of what's hot in your market.

USING KEYWORD STRINGS FROM YOUR METADATA

As we discussed earlier in this book, good keyword strings for your Amazon page are crucial. But these Amazon keywords can also be used in your subtitle, too. And this is why having a subtitle on a book can be good, but also not so good, as I pointed out earlier.

The trick with a good subtitle is that you want something that isn't simply a crammed-together collection of keywords. It needs to make sense as well. In other cases, you want to make sure you're appealing to your reader and what will attract them. For example, using the term, "Clean romance" or "Fast-paced thriller," can help get the attention of key readers. Something like this works:

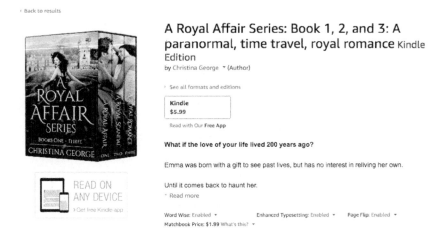

But this next book would probably benefit from a subtitle more geared to pulling in new readers. If you aren't familiar with who Poppy McVie is, you might not be inclined to click on the "buy" button.

As well, this next book has a great, fun cover, but no subtitle, which I think could certainly help improve sales.

Stealing Jason Wilde: A Novel Kindle Edition

by Dee Ernst ˅ (Author)

⭐⭐⭐⭐☆ ˅   138 customer reviews

˅ See all 7 formats and editions

Kindle	Paperback	Audible
$0.00 kindleunlimited	**$6.99**	**$0.00**
This title and over 1 million more available with Kindle Unlimited $1.50 to buy	16 Used from $6.29 21 New from $6.99	Free with your Audible trial

After her divorce, librarian Annie Reynolds thought she'd closed the book on love for good —it just wasn't part of her safe, comfortable routine. But if there's anyplace she can relax and have a little fun, it's Dune Road, where she and her closest girlfriends return for their annual getaway in the Hamptons. She knows it's just what she needs to escape her empty nest (and empty bed).

˅ Read more

BOOK DESCRIPTION

The book description, often overlooked as a means to drive traffic to your page, is also a great place to use keywords and keyword strings. A book description should draw the reader in, but authors tend to get too flowery. Flowery is fine if you're selling fiction, but even then you can still use keyword strings effectively.

Here's a screenshot of the product page for this book, *How to Sell a Truckload of Books on Amazon*. You'll see I use keyword strings throughout the page—in the header, in the description, and in the bullets:

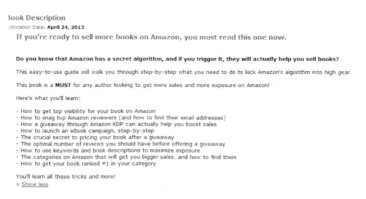

When it comes to fiction, the rules still apply, but you may have to be creative in using your keyword strings. Let's say you find a series of keyword strings like this:

- new romance eBooks
- romance and sex

- romance eBooks
- romance and mystery

It's pretty tough to fit these into a general description if you're sharing things like character details and theme, but you should consider using descriptors that include important keyword strings. Or, if you've used a subtitle, you could also figure out a creative way to repeat it in the book description. If your book description is long enough, you could definitely include some keywords. But using a longer keyword string, such as, "Best new romance eBook," will look awkward and self-aggrandizing.

Instead, consider incorporating a phrase as an additional descriptor in review quotes—*but only if you check with your reviewer/endorser for permission and approval of your rewrite*. For example:

"Loved this book…packed with **romance and sex**!"
"Fantastic buy and among one of the **best new romance eBooks**!"

Do not fail to check with your endorser and ask if it's okay if the review is reworded slightly. Don't redo the entire review; ideally, you should only have to add a word or two to weave in the keyword strings.

Something I've done is add them after the review. If someone writes, "This is a thrill-a-minute ride. I couldn't put it down!" I add, "Sally Reviewer, commenting on this **romance and mystery** book." It can look somewhat awkward, so you'll want to play around with it until it feels and reads right. The bottom line is, weaving in as many keyword phrases/strings as possible can substantially improve your search rank.

Some SEO experts will tell you to use just one string, while others say you should cram all of them into your description. As mentioned, for nonfiction this is pretty simple. Fiction is trickier. Use what feels and reads right; don't overstuff your description just for the sake of inserting keyword strings.

I read one book about Amazon promotion that said you should use your keywords seven times. Frankly, I don't think the number of times matters. It's the nature of the keywords that matters, so spend your time creating a description that utilizes these terms and presents your book in the best possible light. My sense is that, much like the use of author names in keyword strings, Amazon will start cracking down on keyword stuffing in the book description, too—so be careful!

UNDERSTANDING AMAZON ENHANCED CATEGORIES

Your book's categories are extremely important. They're more than simply where your audience will find the book. The more niched, the more specific you can get, the better. This is why I refer to categories as "enhanced," because that's exactly what we're going to dig into in this chapter.

The reality is this: the more narrow your category, the better you'll do on Amazon overall. Much of this has to do with the way the algorithm works. Some nonfiction authors look at bigger categories, like business or social media, and think, "I want to dominate that category!" That is a great goal, but it's often not realistic. If you can dominate a smaller niche category, it will trigger Amazon algorithms, which in turn triggers their internal promotion system. On Amazon, sales breed sales. The more sales you get, the more sales Amazon wants you to get. Digging into niche categories can be another way to trigger this system.

There's a catch, however. Back in May of 2014, categories started changing, mostly in fiction. Previously, an author could choose a super-narrow category like, "Dramas," under "Contemporary romance." But things have changed considerably.

While fiction still has categories, they are more general in nature, and the narrow searches we talked about in the "Keyword String Strategies for Greater Visibility" chapter are accessed with the right keyword strings, but they're also triggered with something called "refined-by themes," which we'll discuss in the next chapter. If you have a fiction book on Amazon and haven't done a lot with it recently, you may want to check which category the book is in, and read through the next chapter carefully. Because if you haven't touched your category in awhile, you can bet Amazon has changed it.

And here's another twist to the story: Amazon is divided into two websites. If you're only doing category research on the main book site, you may be missing out on some great possibilities. My preference is to only do category research in the Amazon Kindle store. Why? Because there are so many new books being published on Amazon, many of them in Kindle format, and that side of Amazon tends to have more variety and better, more narrow results.

Amazon has also changed how many categories you can have. Originally you were allowed to have four, then Amazon dropped it to two. Now you're allowed to have *ten categories*! Why would you want ten? Well it's a great way to get in front of more readers. It's a bit like seeing Starbucks on almost every corner. If you are craving a cup of coffee or a quick bite, you're more likely to go to a Starbucks since they're literally everywhere. The same is true when your book is in multiple categories. It'll show up in more places, in more searches. You get the idea.

With ten categories to work with, you may have to balance between very niche categories and more broad ones. Yes, I said that niche categories are a must—and they are. But if you're trying to get into ten categories, you're bound to find one or two that aren't as narrow as you'd like. That's totally fine. I'd rather be in ten areas than less than ten if I had the option.

When you're trying to decide on which categories make the most sense, it helps to think outside your core market. For example, if you've written a self-help or business book, instead of leaving the book in, "Business," or, "Dieting," two super-huge categories on Amazon, you'll want to put it into something slightly more narrow like the subcategory, "Women and Business," which I'll address in a few pages, where it won't get lost in the onslaught of books dominating these markets. You may also want to mix up your markets; consider what other areas your book might do well in. For example, I have a book called *Red Hot Internet Publicity*, which I put in both the "Business" and "Internet Marketing" sections. Readers might search both areas, so I'm covered.

Be aware that categories can change, and often do—and without notice. Sometimes Amazon even deletes categories. It won't delete your book from the system, but it will delete it from that category—and arbitrarily put it somewhere else.

FINDING THE BEST CATEGORIES ON AMAZON

The Kindle side of Amazon has some great additional categories for your book. Here's how to access it:

1. Go to the Amazon.com search bar and highlight Kindle Store, as in the screenshot below:

2. Then click Go, but do not put a book title in the search bar. Highlighting Kindle Store and clicking Go will drop you into the Kindle side of Amazon, which has a whole different set of categories.

3. Once you're there, click on Kindle eBooks, and voilà, now you can really start digging around. Don't believe me? Have a look at what I found.

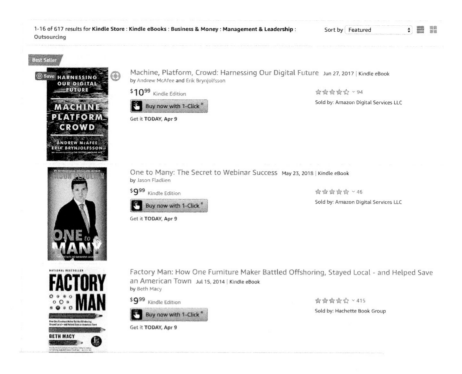

There are a bunch of surprisingly narrow categories, like "Outsourcing," which is under "Business," and which has fewer than 700 books in it. Impressed yet? Check this out. Under "Health/Fitness," I found the subcategory "Teen Health," which had only 320 books in it.

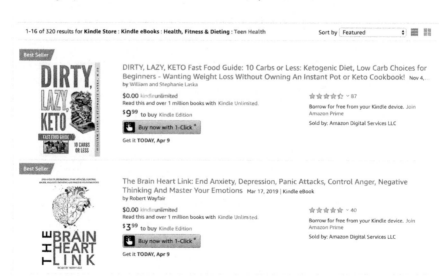

The key here is to keep clicking that bar to the left (see image below) till you find some good places to put your book. As I said earlier, you may not always strike gold with categories that have only 320 books in them, but you'll find many great ones where you can easily add your book!

⟨ Kindle Store
Kindle eBooks
　Arts & Photography
　Biographies & Memoirs
　Business & Money
　Children's eBooks
　Comics, Manga & Graphic
　Novels
　Computers & Technology
　Cookbooks, Food & Wine
　Crafts, Hobbies & Home
　Education & Teaching
　Engineering & Transportation
　Foreign Languages
　Health, Fitness & Dieting
　History
　Humor & Entertainment
　Law
　Lesbian, Gay, Bisexual &
　Transgender eBooks
　Literature & Fiction
　Medical eBooks
　Mystery, Thriller & Suspense
　Nonfiction
　Parenting & Relationships
　Politics & Social Sciences
　Reference
　Religion & Spirituality
　Romance
　Science & Math
　Science Fiction & Fantasy
　Self-Help
　Sports & Outdoors
　Teen & Young Adult
　Travel

CHANGING YOUR CATEGORIES ON AMAZON

When you first publish on Amazon or add your book to their system, they will ask you for the categories where you want your book listed. These are standard industry categories, called BISAC—which everyone from bookstores to specialty stores use. Your categories for your eBook will be different, and we'll change those in a minute. But when you first upload your print and eBook to the system, you'll be stuck with the standard industry categories until you change them. Let's look at how you can make those changes right now.

When you've found the right category for your eBook in the Kindle store, you'll want to make sure your book is added there. You can do this by emailing the links for the categories to Amazon via the Author Central portal. Here's how to do it:

After you click on Help, select Contact us (both circled in red). Once you get there, you'll click the following in this order:

- My Books
- Update information about a book
- Browse categories
- I want to update my book's browse categories

The page will look like this. Be sure to note that you want e-mail contact.

The folks who monitor the Amazon Author Central pages are helpful and efficient. Even if you get the topics you want to contact them about wrong, your e-mail usually ends up in the right place.

Once you're on this screen, you'll want to ask them to move your eBook to the category you specify. When you write them for category changes, I recommend sending them the URL for the category you want, along with the path that's shown on Amazon. So, let's use the Teen Health as an example.

Here's the URL that will take you to that niche within the Amazon website: www.amazon.com/s/ref=lp_156430011_nr_n_15?fst=as %3Aoff&rh=n%3A133140011%2Cn%3A%21133141011%2C n%3A154606011%2Cn%3A156430011%2Cn%3A1171749301 1&bbn=156430011&ie=UTF8&qid=1554842925&rnid=156430011

Next, copy the path that's on the Amazon page. It'll look like this:

Kindle eBooks : Health, Fitness & Dieting : Teen Health

When you email Amazon, you'll put them together like this:

Kindle eBooks : Health, Fitness & Dieting : Teen Health:

www.amazon.com/s/ref=lp_156430011_nr_n_15?fst=as%3Aoff&rh=n%3A133140011%2Cn%3A%211331411011%2Cn%3A154606011%2Cn%3A156430011%2Cn%3A1171749301 1&bbn=156430011&ie=UTF8&qid=1554842925&rnid=156430011

And you'll want to do this for every category you add/change via Author Central. This is a foolproof way to make sure they're putting your book in exactly the right place. Once you email them, it'll take about twenty-four hours before all the changes are made, and that's all you need to do!

REFINE-BY THEMES FOR FICTION

According to Amazon, their refine-by section was implemented for fiction, because consumers were searching for things like the type of protagonist, or where the book was set (beach, city, etc.). It's rumored that Amazon plans to use themes for nonfiction, but as of this writing, I haven't seen this change implemented.

What are refine-by themes? When they were first rolled out, they were considered keywords, meaning additional keywords and strings you could add to your book. Now, however, it's all been changed.

Themes are the new deep-dive categories/keyword strings on Amazon. Let's walk through it.

Refine-by themes are, in general, various aspects of your book's content. For example, if you have a wealthy protagonist, one of your themes would be "Wealthy." If you have a murder mystery with a serial killer, your theme might be "Serial killer." Here's what themes look like on the romance side of the Amazon page:

Refine by

Romantic Heroes

- ☐ Alpha Males
- ☐ BBW
- ☐ Bikers
- ☐ Cowboys
- ☐ Criminals & Outlaws
- ☐ Doctors
- ☐ Firefighters
- ☐ Highlanders
- ☐ Pirates
- ☐ Royalty & Aristocrats
- ☐ Spies
- ☐ Vikings
- ☐ Wealthy

Romantic Themes

- ☐ Amnesia
- ☐ Beaches
- ☐ International
- ☐ Love Triangle
- ☐ Medical
- ☐ Second Chances
- ☐ Secret Baby
- ☐ Vacation
- ☐ Wedding
- ☐ Workplace

You can see a list of "Romantic Themes" and "Romantic Heroes" on the left-hand side of the screen. If you've written a thriller or mystery, you'll have three choices: "Moods & Themes," "Characters," and "Setting."

Refine by

Moods & Themes

- [ ] Action-packed
- [ ] Dark
- [ ] Disturbing
- [ ] Fun
- [ ] Gory
- [ ] Humorous
- [ ] Racy & Risque
- [ ] Romantic
- [ ] Scary
- [ ] Vengeful

Characters

- [ ] Amateur Sleuths
- [ ] British Detectives
- [ ] Gay Protagonists
- [ ] FBI Agents
- [ ] Female Protagonists
- [ ] Lesbian Protagonists
- [ ] Police Officers
- [ ] Private Investigators

Settings

- [ ] Beaches
- [ ] Islands
- [ ] Mountains
- [ ] Outer Space
- [ ] Small Towns
- [ ] Suburban
- [ ] Urban

Staying with the romance theme, let's explore this further. Let's say you have a time travel paranormal romance novel, and it's also got some royals in it. Lots of options here, right?

If you select the themes on the left of the Amazon page, you can narrow your category significantly. Why does that matter? Because the narrower the category, the better it is for your book sales.

It's all about supply and demand: Which theme will end up being high-demand without a lot of supply?

Let's have a look:

Romantic Heroes

‹ Clear
☑ **Royalty & Aristocrats**
☐ Alpha Males
☐ BBW
☐ Cowboys
☐ Doctors
☐ Highlanders
☐ Pirates
☐ Spies
☐ Vikings
☐ Wealthy

Romantic Themes

☐ Amnesia
☐ Beaches
☐ International
☐ Love Triangle
☐ Medical
☐ Second Chances
☐ Secret Baby
☐ Vacation
☐ Wedding
☐ Workplace

Clicking the "Royalty & Aristocrats" gets you into this fun niche with only 231 other books!

1-16 of 231 results for **Kindle Store** : **Kindle eBooks** : **Romance** : **Time Travel** : Royalty & Aristocrats

Now let's have a look at the sales rank of some of these books, to make sure that category is popular. Pay particular attention to the Amazon Best Sellers Rank:

Product details

File Size: 4198 KB
Print Length: 343 pages
Simultaneous Device Usage: Unlimited
Publisher: The Morgan-Stanwood Publishing Group (March 19, 2019)
Publication Date: March 19, 2019
Sold by: Amazon Digital Services LLC
Language: English
ASIN: B07MHQ4MCV
Text-to-Speech: Enabled ⌄
X-Ray: Not Enabled ⌄
Word Wise: Enabled
Lending: Enabled
Screen Reader: Supported ⌄
Enhanced Typesetting: Enabled ⌄
Amazon Best Sellers Rank: #17,360 Paid in Kindle Store (See Top 100 Paid in Kindle Store)
　　　#81 in Time Travel Romance
　　　#93 in Time Travel Romances
　　　#106 in Medieval Historical Romance (Kindle Store)

And this one!

Product details

File Size: 1833 KB
Print Length: 338 pages
Simultaneous Device Usage: Unlimited
Publisher: Carroll Publishing; 2 edition (June 2, 2014)
Publication Date: June 2, 2014
Sold by: Amazon Digital Services LLC
Language: English
ASIN: B00KQ54RNU
Text-to-Speech: Enabled ⌄
X-Ray: Not Enabled ⌄
Word Wise: Enabled
Lending: Enabled
Screen Reader: Supported ⌄
Enhanced Typesetting: Enabled ⌄
Amazon Best Sellers Rank: #13,883 Paid in Kindle Store (See Top 100 Paid in Kindle Store)
　　　#62 in Time Travel Romance
　　　#67 in Action & Adventure Romance (Kindle Store)
　　　#93 in Women's Fantasy Fiction

These are great sales ranks, and probably a great place for your time travel romance book to be sitting.

Just to make sure this is making sense, let's try a different genre. Let's look at, "Mystery." If you hop on over to the Kindle store, click eBooks, then click on, "Mystery, Thriller & Suspense," and then let's refine it by clicking "Crime Fiction":

Department

‹ Kindle Store
‹ Kindle eBooks
‹ Mystery, Thriller & Suspense
  Crime Fiction
     Heist
     Kidnapping
     Murder
     Noir
     Organized Crime
     Serial Killers
     Vigilante Justice

Now you'll see this list of refine-bys, and click "action-packed" and "female protagonist":

Moods & Themes

‹ Clear
☑ **Action-packed**
☐ Dark
☐ Disturbing
☐ Fun
☐ Gory
☐ Humorous
☐ Racy & Risque
☐ Romantic
☐ Scary
☐ Vengeful

Characters

‹ Clear
☑ **Female Protagonists**
☐ Amateur Sleuths
☐ British Detectives
☐ FBI Agents
☐ Lesbian Protagonists
☐ Police Officers
☐ Private Investigators

Settings

☐ Beaches
☐ Islands
☐ Mountains
☐ Small Towns
☐ Suburban
☐ Urban

Take a look at what this gets you:

1-16 of 350 results for **Kindle Store** : **Kindle eBooks** : **Mystery, Thriller & Suspense** : **Crime Fiction** : **Action-packed** : Female Protagonists

Three hundred and fifty books isn't bad. And when I checked the sales ranks for the first three or four, they were all good. So this is definitely a refine-by I'll want to use!

Keep refine-by categories in mind if you decide to spend some time on this technique. By choosing the best refine-by theme/setting/protagonist for your book, you could have it show up in a hot-selling category.

How do you get into these categories? Well, by incorporating the refine-by keywords into the keywords you add to Amazon, or via the KDP dashboard as we discussed, and by using the categories as part of your list of ten categories you want to get into.

And yes, here you'll be using single keywords. This is the one exception to the keyword string rule. When you have the opportunity to associate your book with these refine-by categories, you'll want to stick to seemingly basic keywords like "Noir" and "Serial Killers" from the example above.

In order to get Amazon to niche you into that category and refine-by, you'll have to send them the category string as I mentioned in the previous chapter, and then add the refine-by keywords using your Amazon/KDP Dashboard and perhaps also include them in your book description.

In the case of the Crime Fiction, this is what you'll send to Amazon Author Central:

1-16 of over 50,000 results for Kindle Store : Kindle eBooks : Mystery, Thriller & Suspense : Crime Fiction

www.amazon.com/s?i=digital-text&bbn=6361460011&rh=n%3A133140011%2Cn%3A%21133141011%2Cn%3A154606011%2Cn%3A157305011%2Cn%3A6361460011&dc&fst=as%3Aoff&qid=1554844554&rnid=7130668011&ref=sr_hi_4

Remember, this category only gets you into the Crime Fiction niche.

Then you have to narrow it down using the refine-by keywords, which you can upload to your KDP Dashboard. Be sure NOT to include the refine-bys when you send the Category hyperlink to Author Central, because they'd have to kick it back to you for correction.

Non-fiction has a few refine-by options, specifically for historical periods, but it's pretty minimal to date, so when refine-bys become a more standard option acriss nonfiction categories, I'll be sure to update this book!

HOW TO ACHIEVE MORE VISIBILITY FOR OBSCURE OR NICHE BOOKS

What if you have a book with a limited audience because your topic isn't widely known? How do you drive attention to a book about something that doesn't enjoy popular awareness? The good news is, it's totally possible. And I'm going to tell you how!

Consider the steam mop. Ever heard of it? If not, you may want to get one. Unless you want to keep cleaning your floors with a regular mop that doesn't kill germs. Who wants that? And did you know you can also clean carpets and rugs with a steam mop?

See what I did there? I got you to go from "What the heck is a steam mop?" to "Well, yeah, I want to keep my floors germ-free!"

The idea here is that you need **alignment**, and that's where your keyword strings can take you. Alignment is the concept of bringing together two ideas that aren't obviously related and then connecting them to sell your idea—in this case, your book.

But first you need to find out "where it hurts," or the problem that needs to be solved.

Recently I was doing an Amazon optimization for a book about managing Lyme disease. Now this is kind of a tough market, because it's not a big one. There aren't a ton of Lyme disease books on Amazon.

Reduced competition sounds great, right? In reality, especially Amazon reality, it's not so great in this case, because any books related to hers have a high sales rank. Remember? The bigger the number, the lower the number of books sold.

While I was working on this optimization, I quickly learned it was not very worthwhile to go after "Lyme disease" as a key word. Instead I dug deeper into the illness itself and discovered that it often shows up as other issues—including thyroid problems, arthritis, and other ailments people often search for. The end result was a set of keyword strings that tied the book to those issues. Once we did that, this author was able to boost the overall bounce of the book on Amazon and get it in front of readers who might want to consider other options for disease management.

The thing about this strategy—and this is specific to nonfiction—is that you need to make sure your book description matches and is aligned with this train of thought. In the Lyme disease author's case, I suggested she update the book description to include these other ailments, with the goal of a reader seeing it and saying, "Oh, I hadn't considered that!"

I followed this same process with a book about teen bullying as it relates to teen suicide. Of course it comes up against one of the two things we Americans never like to talk about: death and whether we've saved enough for retirement.

But this author had her book in the death/suicide category and used the keyword strings "Teen suicide" and, "Suicide." Needless to say, her book wasn't doing well. I suggested that she switch the book to the "Teen health," category, which had very few competing titles, plus it had great sales ranks.

Note: This is the important difference between low numbers in a category or keyword string search. If you have low competition and a low sales rank (low means you're selling a ton of books) that's golden!

Additionally, I recommended to this author that she remove all references to death and suicide from her keyword strings and instead focus on what parents might be interested in related to her message. We used new terms like "bullying" and "helping my teen," which were far more popular.

The key idea is to turn your book into the end of the road in terms of their needs. Show them that, whether they want to be entertained, educated, or enlightened, your book is what they need.

However, in order to get them there, you have to meet them much earlier down their path of discovery.

Most authors choose keyword strings, book descriptions, and categories that are too far down the road to reach their readers—that is, too close to the end decision.

If you can reach them earlier, you can present your book without a huge crowd of competing distractions and gain new readers. You'll be surprised how well this works.

And while it's a tad less obvious, the same is true for boosting visibility of any fiction book. Tying your book to ideas your readers may be interested in—paranormal elements, specific settings, or other book attributes, can help you gain more real estate in those vital search areas.

HOW GREAT AMAZON BOOK DESCRIPTIONS HELP INDIE AUTHORS SELL MORE BOOKS

Whether we're talking about Amazon, or any other e-tailer, book descriptions are more important than most authors realize.

Too many times I'll see blocks of text pulled from the back of the book. In theory, it's not the worst idea. However, it may not be the greatest idea if your book description isn't strong to begin with, or if the book details are just slapped up on Amazon—or Barnes & Noble, iTunes and so on—without giving an eye to things like spacing, bulleting, shorter paragraphs, and boldface.

In this section we'll discuss some ideas about book descriptions specifically, and then review some tips you may want to consider in order to enhance your own book description for maximum effectiveness on Amazon.

IS YOUR BOOK DESCRIPTION MEMORABLE WHETHER IT'S SCANNED OR READ WORD-FOR-WORD?

Most people don't read websites; they scan. The same is true for your book description. If you have huge blocks of text without any consideration for spacing, boldface, bulleted lists, short paragraphs, or some other form of highlighting that helps the reader scan, it's unlikely to attract readers. When your description is visually and psychologically appealing, it invites the reader to delve in instead of click off.

Book design, meaning the actual font on the pages, adopts this strategy, too. By having wide margins (referred to as gutters in the book design world) and spacing, and, in nonfiction, bulleted lists and even boxed-in pieces to highlight particular text, you invite the reader to read instead of doing a quick scan and rushing on.

Our minds are image processors, not text processors, so huge pieces of text that fill a page overwhelm the mind and, in fact, slow down the processing time considerably.

When we're looking at websites, our attention span is even shorter than it is while reading a book. Even sites like Amazon—where consumers go to buy, and often spend a lot of time comparing products and reading reviews—it's important to keep in mind that most potential readers will move on if your description is too cumbersome.

HOW CAN YOU MAKE YOUR DESCRIPTION MORE SCAN-FRIENDLY?

- **Headlines**: The first sentence in the description should be a grabber, something that pulls the reader in. This text could also be an enthusiastic review quote or some other kind of endorsement, but regardless, it should be bolded. In the case of your Amazon book page, you could also use the "Amazon Orange" to set your headline apart from the rest of the text.
- **Paragraphs**: Keep paragraphs short at 2-3 sentences max.
- **Bolding**: You can boldface key text throughout the description. In fact, I recommend it. Just be sure you aren't using boldface too much. Don't highlight two or three sentences in bold, because it'll have more impact if you do just one sentence or a few keyword strings.
- **Bullets or Numbers**: If your book is nonfiction, it can be very effective to bullet or number as much of your information as possible. Take key points and the "here's what you'll learn" elements and put them into a bullet point/numbering section that's easy to scan and visually appealing.

USE CODE TO ENHANCE YOUR AMAZON BOOK DESCRIPTION AND HEADLINE

How do you spruce up the text styles within your book description? There are several types of code you can use to enhance your headline and description. Keep in mind that you can't make these changes to your headline via Author Central; it all has to be done from the KDP Dashboard. Although this won't affect your algorithm per se, it will help make your book description more visually appealing.

Here are some of the coding enhancers available:

- **Bolding**: The text you want bolded
- *Italics*: <i>The text you want italicized</i>
- Headline: <h1>The text you want for a headline</h1>
- Amazon Orange Headline: <h2>The text you want for a headline in Amazon Orange</h2>

You can add in numbered lists and bullet points, too.

ANSWERING READERS' MOST IMPORTANT QUESTION: "WHAT'S IN IT FOR ME?"

The biggest challenge authors face is writing a book description that effectively highlights the book's benefits for readers. This matters whether it's fiction or nonfiction, and it's a crucial part of any book description.

Remember, with 4,500 books published every day in this country, you can't afford to have a vague, meandering book description. You must state clearly why your book is the best one they can buy.

This leads us to the differences between fiction and nonfiction when it comes to book descriptions.

NONFICTION

First off, it's probably very likely that whomever you're targeting already owns a few titles similar to the one you just wrote. Then why on earth should they add yours to their collection?

While you're powering through your book description, keep in mind that you're likely serving a very cluttered market. You need to be precise and vividly clear about why your book matters. You should hook the reader from the first sentence, and remember to make a personal connection with the reader via the book description.

Nonfiction shoppers are more often than not looking for the solution to a problem. They're not browsing for their next beach read. So your book description needs to *zero in on what that problem likely is*, plus they need to feel like you understand them, and they need to be convinced you're the best person to help them work through it.

And if you're a noted expert in your field, with accolades to back it up, work those in briefly, because in this day and age it truly does set you apart. So do reviews by other experts in your field or industry, but keep them short and sweet—excerpts of the best parts are plenty. Save your full bio and complete reviews for the other sections Amazon gives you.

FICTION

Fiction is a bit tougher, because it's easy to reveal too much, or not quite enough. For this reason, I encourage you to focus on developing your elevator pitch (see below), because that's going to be your cliffhanger, or your readers' key interest point in the book. Every other piece of the story anchors to that.

When it comes to fiction, buyers have a lot of options, so be clear about what your book is about, and lead with the hook. Your opening sentence should be the best you've got—because it might be the only chance you get. And don't confuse not giving it all away with being vague. If you're vague, the potential reader won't experience the emotional connection they need in order to make them want to find out more. So give them a story arc to latch onto and leave them needing more.

Keep movie trailers in mind while you're writing your fiction description. They often do an outstanding job of giving enough of the story to get you hooked without revealing so much it prevents you from watching it.

CHILDREN'S AND/OR YOUNG ADULT TITLES

For these books, make sure to include the intended age range. Even though you can add it in the Amazon details, I've had parents tell me that seeing it in the book description is incredibly helpful, because if anyone is short on time and needs help making smart buying decisions, it's parents. It also helps a lot to let them know right away what their child will learn, or what discussions or themes the book will highlight. And remember, while you wrote the book for children, you're selling it to adults, so don't oversimplify your description, thinking you're off the hook. Adjust your approach to reach parents who are short on time. They'll buy what seems like a sure thing, which leaves very little room for error.

DEVELOPING YOUR ELEVATOR PITCH

What is an elevator pitch, and why do you need one?

An elevator pitch is a one- to two-sentence description of your book. It's the briefest of the brief descriptions you will develop. Elevator pitches are important because we have ever-shrinking attention spans, and there are times when you need to capture someone's attention with a very short, succinct pitch.

And why does this matter for your book description? Because having a short hook is an excellent way to start building your book description. Also, elevator pitches focus on the core of your book—the one element that your book could not be without—and that's what matters most to your reader.

KEEP YOUR WORDING SIMPLE

When it comes to writing a book description, I encourage you to save your five-dollar words for another time. Book descriptions that work well tend to use simple language that any layperson can understand. If you make someone pause to think about a word, you'll lose them, and the effectiveness of your book description will go right out the window.

But don't underestimate the power of a thesaurus. While you may want to repeat a few lucrative keyword strings, you don't want too much repetition because it will get boring. Great public speakers don't use the same words over and over again, because they understand the importance of creating good sound bites, and they're smart about choosing words that aren't overused. This is a winning strategy for creating something memorable that stands out from the competition.

HOW EXCITED ARE YOU? AND HOW EXCITED WILL YOUR READERS BE?

Have you ever seen a book description with a ton of exclamation points or all caps? Much like in an e-mail, it feels like the writer is screaming at you. Although I don't recommend eliminating exclamation points entirely from your book description, they should be used sparingly. I'd recommend one or two at most. Studies have shown that an exclamation point used here and there can help make a sentence seem even more emphatic.

In terms of all caps, don't even bother. Using all caps, even for a word or two or a single sentence in a book description, makes you look like an amateur.

SPELL CHECK

Doing a spell check should go without saying, yet still I've seen enough descriptions loaded with typos that I feel like I need to say it. Please don't put up a book description full of typos. Even one is too many.

IS YOUR BOOK PART OF A SERIES?

If your book is one in a series, be sure to tell readers, and add it right in the headline. I also recommend that you make it part of the title, too. For example, you might word your book title like this: *Deadly Heat: Heat Series, Book 4 of 7.*

Here's an example of Dan Silva's book title, which is a good illustration of putting series information in the actual book title:

The Black Widow (Gabriel Allon Series Book 16)
Kindle Edition
by Daniel Silva ▾ (Author)

I recommend doing this because readers, especially fiction readers, love a series. Tell them right up front that your book is part of an ongoing or similar story.

INCLUDE TOP KEYWORDS

Keywords are as important to your Amazon book page as almost anything else. I've written a lot about Amazon-specific keyword strings that you can see on our blog called (Demystifying Amazon Categories, Themes, and Keywords—Part 1 and Part 2), but here's a quick overview:

The term "keyword" is actually inaccurate, because readers don't search based on a single keyword. Think instead of keyword strings.

For example, "Romance about second chances" or "Second-chance romances," have been popular search strings on Amazon for a while now. However, by taking that sentence and inserting it into your book description, you can help boost your visibility on the site, as well as keying into your readers' specific interest. If they're searching for, "Romance second chances," and they see it in your book description, it's going to ping them with: "Oh! This is the exact book I've been looking for."

That said, it's a good idea to avoid overstuffing your book description with keywords. I recommend finding six or seven strings and using them sparingly throughout.

You can read the full blog posts here: www.amarketingexpert.com/demystifying-amazon-categories-themes-and-keywords-part-1-of-2/

www.amarketingexpert.com/demystifying-amazon-categories-themes-and-keywords-part-2-of-2/

DON'T MARKET TO YOUR EGO

I often say to authors, "No one cares that you wrote a book." And while family and friends may care, they aren't your target audience. If you want to pull in readers—a lot of them—make sure your book appeals to *their* needs and *their* interests, not *yours*. This is partially why I never recommend that authors write their own book descriptions. I often hire someone to do it for me, because I'm just too close to it to see what might *really matter* to my reader.

TAILOR YOUR BIO TO YOUR BOOK

One of things I see a lot is author bio information that has nothing to do with the book. For example, let's say you wrote a book about marriage, but your bio talks about how you live in Maine with your wife and three dogs. That doesn't help convince readers of your expertise for writing this book.

The same is true for fiction. If you've published multiple books, mention it. If you have a fun or quirky writing habit, mention that, too. It's a good idea to tailor your bio for your audience and the market.

And, especially with nonfiction, list any credentials as they may relate to the book topic and/or any research you've done. Most of all, make it interesting and *keep it short*. Long, boring author bios don't sell books.

INCLUDE QUOTES AND REVIEWS

So often I see quotes such as, "This is the best mystery book I've read in ages!" But who actually said it is left out. Reviews and quotes/blurbs are fantastic to use in your book description, *but only if they are properly cited*.

Several authors have told me they often don't cite reviews because they feel the reviewer's name won't lend the kind of credibility they want for the blurb—for example, a quote from someone at work or a neighbor. In this case, why not ask them to review the book via the Amazon/Barnes&Noble/ iTunes/etc. site instead?

GET A SECOND OPINION

We're often too close to our own work to fully wrap our minds around what the market wants from us. From my own experience I can tell you it's a delicate balance between teaching authors what I feel they need to learn, and discussing problems they want me to address.

So I'd encourage you to use your editor's help for your book description, or get some feedback from other trusted individuals who know your market really well, and take their suggestions and edits to heart.

UPDATE YOUR PAGE OFTEN

Here's something you may not have considered: Your page isn't set in cement. In fact, ideally it shouldn't be static. When you get good reviews and awards, update your book page to reflect that. When you do your keyword string and category research every quarter (yep, put it on the list) consider whether there are any new ones you can sprinkle throughout the different sections on Author Central.

And here's another idea. If you're doing a special promotion, book promo, discount, or whatever, why not mention it in your book description? (See screenshot below.)

Finally, take a look at the book description below from Dan Silva. It's a great example of a blurb that combines great review quotes with a book description that pulls you in from the first sentence.

Book blurbs are eye candy, because people like what other people like. Even if you don't have review quotes from highly respected or recognizable publications such as *Booklist* and *Publishers Weekly*, you should still add reviews. Just be sure to cite them correctly.

Notice how they are boldfaced to draw attention to them? And check out the second paragraph. Whoever wrote this book description inserted a review to help bolster the character description, which is another clever idea.

"Fascinating, suspenseful, and bated-breath exciting.... Silva proves once again that he can rework familiar genre material and bring it to new life."
— *Publishers Weekly*, starred review

"Silva builds suspense like a symphony conductor.... A winner on all fronts."
— *Booklist*, starred review

Bestselling author Daniel Silva delivers another spellbinding international thriller—one that finds the legendary Gabriel Allon grappling with an ISIS mastermind.

Gabriel Allon, the art restorer, spy, and assassin described as the most compelling fictional creation "since Ian Fleming put down his martini and invented James Bond" (*Rocky Mountain News*), is poised to become the chief of Israel's secret intelligence service. But on the eve of his promotion, events conspire to lure him into the field for one final operation. ISIS has detonated a massive bomb in the Marais district of Paris, and a desperate French government wants Gabriel to eliminate the man responsible before he can strike again.

Book descriptions, whether on Amazon, iTunes, or Barnes & Noble, are your sales pitch. Ultimately, descriptions will or won't sell your book, so make sure yours is tightly written, exceptionally engaging, and most of all, turns a browse into a buy.

HOW TO WRITE A KICK-ASS AMAZON BIO TO SELL MORE BOOKS

Authors often don't spend enough time crafting their bios. Most of them write up a quick "about me" and never give it a second thought. They either treat it like a resume, and risk boring readers to death, or they treat it like a throwaway and it makes zero sense for their topic or genre.

The problem with this tactic is, you're missing an opportunity to drive sales on Amazon and other sites.

In fact, as I look over author bios, I continue to be surprised by how many are lackluster. Sure, they talk about the author, but mostly about their hobbies, where they live, and how they like to pass the time when they aren't writing.

If this describes your bio, then this section is for you, especially if you write nonfiction. It's time to make your bio into a killer sales driver on Amazon. Here's how!

START WITH AN OUTLINE AND ALL BOOK TIE-INS

Before you begin, create a list or an outline of everything you've done related to the book. This can include research, work you've done in a related industry, accreditations, lectures and classes you've conducted, other books you've written, or awards you've won. You may want to include some of these elements, but not all of them. The rest of these bullets will help you determine which to include.

IT'S NOT ABOUT YOU

Remember that while we start out by focusing on you and your achievements, this bio actually isn't about you. It's about your reader and knowing what your prospective audience is looking for.

Let's take a look at Mark Shaefer's bio, which I found on Amazon. His bio is keenly focused on his expertise as it relates to the book. Having read Mark's other books and seen him speak, I can tell you he probably has a lot more he could have added to this, but he kept it short and relevant to the book.

About the Author
Mark W. Schaefer is a globally-recognized author, speaker, podcaster, and business consultant who blogs at {grow} — one of the top five marketing blogs of the world. He teaches graduate marketing classes at Rutgers University and has written five best-selling books including The Tao of Twitter (the best-selling book on Twitter in the world) and The Content Code, named by INC magazine as one of the Top five marketing books of the year. Mark also wrote the classic first book on influence marketing, Return On Influence. His many global clients include Pfizer, Cisco, Dell, Adidas, and the US Air Force. He has been a keynote speaker at prestigious events all over the world including SXSW, Marketing Summit Tokyo, and the Institute for International and European Affairs. He has appeared as a guest on media channels such as CNN, The Wall Street Journal, The New York Times and CBS News.

WRITE IN THIRD PERSON

When it comes to writing a bio, never use words like "I" and "me," because a bio written in first person is an awkward read.

SHOW THE READER YOUR EXPERTISE—BE CREDIBLE

There's nothing wrong with being a first-time author. When it comes to the credible portion of this bio you are creating or reworking, this may seem tricky. But remember, this is where your initial work comes in. How long have you been writing? Did you utilize any special techniques or resources in this book?

Check out Pete Ryan's bio. He's a first-time author, but he leads this bio with his background as a journalist, which tells the reader he is an experienced writer. Pete is also a marketing guy and has a successful business in So Cal. You'll notice he doesn't even mention it, because it won't matter to his readers, and Pete knows this.

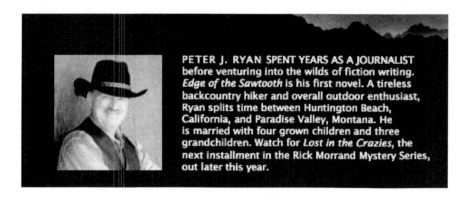

PETER J. RYAN SPENT YEARS AS A JOURNALIST before venturing into the wilds of fiction writing. *Edge of the Sawtooth* is his first novel. A tireless backcountry hiker and overall outdoor enthusiast, Ryan splits time between Huntington Beach, California, and Paradise Valley, Montana. He is married with four grown children and three grandchildren. Watch for *Lost in the Crazies*, the next installment in the Rick Morrand Mystery Series, out later this year.

ADD KEYWORD STRINGS PARTICULAR TO AMAZON

As you already know, keyword strings matter greatly on Amazon. If you've already done your keyword string research, add them to your Amazon bio, too.

You don't have to worry about re-working your book cover to include your keyword strings, because it only matters on Amazon. How many should you include in your bio? As many as you can include authentically without making it awkward and difficult to read. Don't cram your bio full of keywords just for the sake of having them there.

Why does this matter? I've talked about how Amazon is a search engine. Like a search engine, Amazon will "spider" or "crawl" our book page for keyword strings, so make sure at least one or two of the ones you've found are in your bio.

BE PERSONAL (IF APPROPRIATE)

There's a time and a place for a personal-type bio. One is when you've written about something that's been a personal struggle for you, such as a memoir. J.D. Vance's book (released in 2016) features a great example of a bio that's a bit more personal. You'll see he talks a bit less about his experience and more about his personal background, where he lives, his wife, and his dogs.

More about the author

› Visit Amazon's Vance, J. D. Page

Biography

J.D. Vance grew up in the Rust Belt city of Middletown, Ohio, and the Appalachian town of Jackson, Kentucky. He enlisted in the Marine Corps after high school and served in Iraq. A graduate of the Ohio State University and Yale Law School, he has contributed to the National Review and is a principal at a leading Silicon Valley investment firm. Vance lives in San Francisco with his wife and two dogs.

Amazon Author Rank beta (What's this?)

#50 Overall (See top 100 authors)

#2 in Books › Biographies & Memoirs

#50 in Books

+ Follow

BE FUNNY (IF APPROPRIATE)

Be like what you wrote about. That means if your book is funny, then be funny. Check out this bio from Karen Alpert. Her book is *I Heart My Little A-Holes: A bunch of holy-crap moments no one ever told you about parenting.*

From the Publisher

Karen Alpert

There are a Lot of Reasons I Wrote This Book, I Mean, Besides Money by Karen Alpert

When I had my daughter I remember looking down at my newborn and thinking there's a reason God made babies ridiculously cute. So we wouldn't give them away. Or eat them. Because having a kid is like the hardest thing on earth. I mean yeah it's super rewarding and you can't help but loving them to pieces, but no one ever tells you before you have kids just how difficult it's going to be. And you'd never know it from looking at Facebook or Pinterest. You'd think that having kids is all hunky dory and awesome and smiley, like unicorns flying over rainbows. Wait, unicorns don't fly. Fine, unicorns with wings. But I digress. So this is why I wrote this book. To let parents everywhere know that they are not alone. That parenting is hard for everyone. Being preggers, breastfeeding, tantrums, explosive blowout diapers, bedtimes, naptimes, scraping projectile vomit off the ceiling, scraping projectile poop off the wall, the terrible twos, the terrible threes, the terrible fours, etc etc etc. Okay, pardon me while I get all serious for a moment here. Picture a mom who just had a baby for the first time. Her hormones are bouncing off the walls like a pinball machine that's being played by a kid who just chugged four Red Bulls, her nipples feel like they're being eaten by fire ants, and her new baby hasn't let her sleep more than two straight hours in the past three weeks. This little tiny being is constantly with her, and yet she's never felt so alone. This is the reason I wrote this book. Picture a mom standing in the middle of a supermarket where her kid is literally going cuckoo for Cocoa Puffs because she won't buy them, and everyone in the store is staring at her like she is the worst parent on earth. This is the reason I wrote this book. Picture a mom looking at the clock figuring out that she has exactly 84 minutes until her husband comes home from work. Or a dad knowing he has exactly 176 days until his wife comes home from Afghanistan. Or a mom doing it all alone day after day after day because she's single. This is the reason I wrote this book. Kids are awesome. We love them to death and once we have them we can't imagine life without them. But they're also little a-holes who torture us on a daily basis and make us feel like we're doing it all wrong. This is the reason I wrote this book. To make people laugh and feel a little less alone in the impossible, awesome, horrendous, amazing, challenging, exciting, disgusting, unbelievable job of being a parent.

SHORT IS THE NEW LONG

The days of bios that rival the length of your book are gone. Keep it short because, while people do care who wrote the book, they don't care enough to read paragraphs upon paragraphs about you. Save the long one for your website, the foundation of your infrastructure, and where readers will go when they want to learn even more about you!

INCLUDE A CALL TO ACTION & HOW READERS CAN FIND YOU

Do you want your readers to take any action besides buying your book? Are you giving something away on your website? Or do you have an exclusive reader group you want to invite readers to join? Want them to join your newsletter? Then mention it in your bio. Also, be sure to add your website address so they can find you.

Now your bio is ready to rock on Amazon. As an indie author, you'll find that this is invaluable, not only for your book marketing, but also for your book sales. Invest the time now, and you'll have something solid to build on when you publish more books. And remember that bullet list? Keep it handy. You never know when you'll need it for future projects and books!

CUSTOMIZE IT & CHANGE IT UP

Is there something going on in the world that ties into your book? Then mention it. Change up your bio. You can change your Amazon bio as often as you want, and don't forget the algorithms notice and respond when a book page is updated.

And if you're reading this and you're with a traditional publisher, you may be thinking, "They won't let me change my bio!" Trust me, you don't need your publisher to make changes. Just do it on your Amazon Author Central dashboard and—voilà—done and done.

You should also modify your bio when you win awards, get more mentions, or get some fab new reviews. For example, *"The New York Times calls this book 'groundbreaking…'"* is a review quote you could easily add at the end of your bio for a strong finish.

Your bio should be a fluid extension of your author brand, so set your calendar to ensure you review it once a month if you're busy, or at least once a quarter if you're just starting out. This may seem like a lot, but it serves another purpose: it gets your eyes on your entire book page, and once you're there, hopefully you're inspired to cast a critical eye on other areas and make updates that could help drive some more sales.

AMAZON BOOK PRICING TIPS

Book pricing is another way you can activate the Amazon system to boost your ranking.

First, however, it's important to understand the Amazon royalty system. When you publish through KDP, you can choose either a 35% or a 70% royalty. Initially you might say 70% is a no-brainer. But there's more to it than you might think.

Amazon has a "sweet spot" when it comes to pricing. The highest-rated eBooks are generally priced between $2.99 and $5.99. This doesn't mean you won't see higher-priced books in top categories, but they typically will bounce up there for a short period of time and then vanish. Consistent sales require better, smarter pricing, especially for first-time authors.

A lot of folks price their books based on word count. While there's some merit to this, keep in mind that if you price your book over $5.00, you could be pricing yourself out of the market, especially if you're an indie.

There's another element to book pricing, and that's changing the price point of your book on a semi-regular basis. You could have a $0.99 sale, or make it free for an eBook promotion. You can drop the price of the book for a week during launch time to help boost your algorithm results.

My point is, your price doesn't have to remain static. You can reduce it when you run specials, promote new books, and more. This doesn't mean you should change the price of your book daily, or even weekly. But if you have more than one book, you can certainly have at least one of them on sale all the time.

Generally, if an author has three or more titles, I recommend they rotate them in terms of pricing. I suggest this because it helps your Amazon algorithm. Changing the price of one book a month isn't frequent enough, and you'll end up training your potential buyers to simply wait for the lower price. However, keeping your books at one stagnant price is never a good idea if you want to increase your market/reader numbers.

HOW TO BOOST YOUR BOOK WITH AMAZON'S PRE-ORDER

As many of you probably already know, Amazon now allows eBook pre-orders for KDP authors, which essentially levels the playing field between traditionally published authors and those who self-publish through KDP. I'll take you through the steps to get your book into pre-order, but first let's look at when and how this may benefit you.

On Amazon's Kindle Pre-Order information page, they say that pre-orders are great for building buzz. True. But there is a caveat. Over the years, I've found that pre-orders aren't as effective when you have no fan base, and even then they're iffy. What's the real benefit to pre-order? Here's the breakdown:

NEWLY PUBLISHED

If you're a newly published author, the idea of a pre-order seems super enticing, right? Your book is up on the Amazon site as time ticks toward its release. It *is* pretty exciting, but don't spend a ton of time marketing your pre-order page at this point. No one knows you (yet), so marketing efforts may be a waste of time. You can do a small push to friends and family and to a mailing list if you have one, but at this point it's smarter to start playing with categories and keyword strings to see what spikes the book and what doesn't, so you'll be ready to go on launch day.

ALREADY PUBLISHED

If you have a book out there (or several), and you've built a mailing list of fans, then pre-order can build excitement for your upcoming book. But most, if not all, of your marketing should be reserved for when the book is available on Amazon, because that will benefit you so much more.

Unless you are JK Rowling or some other mega-best seller, it's not easy to drive significant numbers to your pre-order page. The other issue you run into is if a reader wants something now, they may not want to wait for your book to be ready and could end up buying something else instead. That said, pre-order can be a lot of fun for fans who've been waiting for your next book.

LONG VERSUS SHORT

Regardless of the category you're in, don't stretch the pre-order time to the full 90 days Amazon allows. Because if you aren't spending a ton of time promoting the book, you don't want it up too long. I'd recommend a month. Also, be sure to hit the deadline you assign the pre-order, because once you select it, as we'll see shortly, you can't go back. Pick a date you know you can hit. As of this printing, Amazon penalizes authors who miss their pre-order date.

PROMOTION

To promote a pre-order, buzz it to your followers and your e-mail list. Again, if this is your second, third, or fourth book, interest is going to be stronger than with your first. Still, you can start to drive some interest to the book, or at least let your friends, family, and followers know it's coming. You can use your cover or other images on Facebook posts, Twitter updates, blog posts, Amazon Ads and so on. But make sure it's all part of the entire conversation, not the only discussion you're having with your followers. Meaning, don't just spend your time pushing your book to your followers, because that will get old fast and lose you buyers. When we get to the chapters about promotions later in this book, we'll dig into some things you can do to help boost your pre-order sales, too!

REVIEWS

Keep in mind that readers can't review a pre-order book. If you're looking to get some early reviews, consider focusing on Goodreads, where you can push for pre-order reviews and provide what are called ARCs (advance reader copies) to potential reviewers.

PRICING YOUR PRE-ORDER

As mentioned earlier, there's a sweet spot in pricing. I would keep it low, even if you plan to raise the price later. You're competing with millions of titles on Amazon, and your book isn't even out yet. If you want to entice an impulse buy, keep the pricing low at first. Once the book is live, you can always raise the price.

THE AMAZON ALGORITHM FOR PRE-ORDERS

There's a certain amount of momentum that a book captures, just organically, when it launches on Amazon. It sits in the "new release" section of Amazon, which can be a great spot to garner additional interest. But if your book is on pre-order and then hits the Amazon system on launch day with little to no buzz, no reviews, and no activity, it'll quickly plummet down into the high sales rank (low sales) numbers. In order to avoid this kind of oblivion, you do need to plan a solid promotional campaign for the book the day it launches—and again, we'll cover this later on in the book!

HOW TO SET UP YOUR PRE-ORDER

First and foremost, you need to be a KDP author. Your eBook should be uploaded into the KDP system via their author/book dashboard. Once you're there, you'll see this:

Pre-order

Once you select a date, the system will tell you that you must get the final book to Amazon no later than four days prior. Additionally, you need to upload a manuscript for them to approve before they'll set up your pre-order. The manuscript doesn't have to be pre-edited; they just want to see what you plan to publish. You'll need a cover, but it doesn't have to be final either. If you're still a month out with no cover (it happens more often than you think), you can leave the cover blank or put up a placeholder, then add your cover before the pre-order goes live. Here's what the page looks like when it's launched on their site:

According to Amazon, the book can be any length, so if you've written a novella, you can use pre-order, too. Right now there are no limitations, other than that you need to be a KDP author, and, if you're an indie author, this is for eBooks only.

Pre-order is a fun, cool option for self-published authors, but be mindful of how much of your promotional sweat equity and money you spend. Most readers prefer to buy a book they can read right away. The urge for instant gratification is especially true for eBook readers, because for them it truly is instant.

HACKING AMAZON'S AD SYSTEM

When Amazon first launched their ads about two years ago, many authors jumped on the Amazon ad-system bandwagon. The ads seemed simple enough, and the results seemed pretty darned good.

Soon enough, however, Amazon realized it was onto something even bigger, and Amazon Marketing Services (AMS) was born. Now, in 2019, Amazon is actively looking to compete with Google in terms of ad systems—and, as you'll see from this chapter, they're getting very close to it.

Let's dig in.

WHAT KIND OF ADS CAN YOU CREATE?

Within the Amazon ad system, there are two types of ads you can create for books:

1. Sponsored Product Ads
2. Lock Screen Ads

Sponsored ads show up like the two screenshots below:

Sponsored products related to this item (What's this?)

And Then She Was GONE	Marked by Love: A Zodiac	Unscripted: A Second	Green Eyes and Good
Christopher Greyson	Shifters Paranormal	Chance Hollywood	Hair
Grab your copy of this	Romance: Taurus	Romance	Hugh O. Smith
brand new novel in the	Rosalie Redd	Lisa Swallow	*She wants a good time, no*
wildly-popular Detective	*When you're marked by*	*Are you ready to meet*	*strings. He's a player who*
Jack Stratton Series and	*love, you can't outrun the*	*British bad boy Tate*	*thinks she's an easy target.*
start reading this	*past. "Exceptionally*	*Daniels?A sizzling second*	*Each has an agenda, then*
electrifying whodunit	*written, absolutely*	*chance Hollywood*	*something happens that*
today!	*recommended."*	*romance.New Release.*	*changes them both.*
⭐⭐⭐⭐☆ 2,185	⭐⭐⭐⭐⭐ 27	*Available on Kindle*	⭐⭐⭐⭐☆ 50
Kindle Edition	Kindle Edition	*Unlimited.*	Kindle Edition
$0.99	$2.99	⭐⭐⭐⭐☆ 23	$4.99
		Kindle Edition	
		$2.99	

These ads can appear in searches or on a book's product/sales page in a row at the bottom.

Amazon Lockscreen ads currently only show up on Kindle devices, meaning that your ad won't show unless your reader has an actual Kindle device. This may make a difference in whether or not you opt to do these ads, mostly due to reader demographics. For example, genre fiction readers in general tend to read on an actual Kindle vs. the Kindle app on an iPad or other make of tablet.

To give you an idea of what Lockscreen ads look like, here's an example from Amazon which outlines how these will show up:

Where your ads may appear on Amazon devices:

| Full-screen ad on locked Kindle E-reader. | Banner ad on the Kindle E-reader homepage. | Full-screen ad on Fire tablet in full-color display. |

When readers tap your ad, they are sent to your book's detail page, where they can easily purchase and download your title.*

You can start reaching eBook readers by copying your eligible Product Display Ads to Lockscreen Ads, or you can create new Lockscreen Ads using the steps below.

For the purposes of this chapter, I'm going to focus on Sponsored Product Ads, since my testing of the Lockscreen Ads wasn't great. I found it difficult to get books approved into this particular ad segment, and once I did, the ROI just wasn't there. I suspect Amazon has rolled these out in Beta, and I'll update this chapter as these ads start to become more user-friendly.

TIPS AND TRICKS FOR GREAT ADS

SETTING UP YOUR ADS

In the fall of 2018 Amazon rolled out some massive changes to their AMS dashboard, most of which have been great. But it's taken a bit of time to test and figure out the best process, which I'll share with you here.

First, let's look at the basics of setting up an ad.

To get started on your AMS ads, head on over to the AMS dashboard here: www.ams.amazon.com/. Log in using your Amazon account details, and the program will take you through the Amazon ad setup process.

Advertising Campaigns

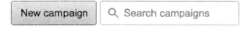

Campaign metrics may take up to 3 days to appear and do not include Kindle Unlimited

When you click "new campaign" and select Sponsored Products, this screen will pop up:

Create campaign

Settings

Campaign name

Example: Holiday Favorites

Start

Apr 10, 2019

End

No end date

Choosing no end date means your campaign will run longer, and a longer timeframe can give you better insights on search terms and keyword performance to further optimize your campaign.

Daily budget

$

Most campaigns with a budget over $5.00 run throughout the day.

Targeting

○ Automatic targeting
Amazon will target keywords and products that are similar to the product in your ad. Learn more

Use this strategy when you are first getting started or want to launch a campaign quickly.

○ Manual targeting
Choose keywords or products to target shopper searches and set custom bids. Learn more

Use this strategy when you know which keywords deliver the most value for your business.

Ad format

○ Custom text ad
Add custom text to your ad to give customers a glimpse of the book. Limit one product per campaign.

○ Standard ad
Choose this option to advertise your products without custom text.

As you start to set it up, you'll see under Targeting that you can choose Automatic targeting or Manual targeting. I always choose Manual so I can add in my own keyword strings. Amazon's system is good, but I'm not confident that they'll pick the exact right keyword strings for my book.

For Ad Format, I'm recommending that you select "Custom text ad" and create your own ad within the template they provide for you.

You'll then scroll down to see this screen:

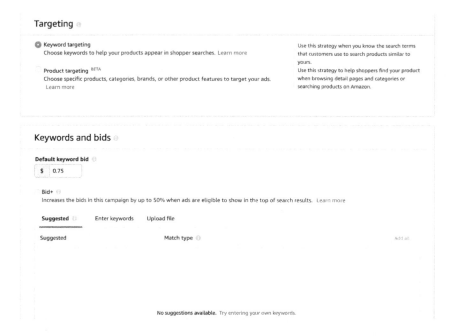

This gives you the option of selecting Keyword targeting or Product targeting. For now, let's go with Keyword targeting, and I'll walk you through finding your exact right keyword strings in a minute.

In terms of "Default keyword bid," I recommend starting at .50 a click, and make sure that Bid+ box is unchecked, unless you want Amazon to randomly increase your keyword bids for you. You can probably play with that feature later, but while you're getting your feet wet in this system, I recommend monitoring it on your own until you get the hang of which keyword strings are doing well versus those that aren't.

AD BUDGET AND CPC

To start out, I recommend that you start with a $10 a day daily budget and $0.50 cost per click (CPC). You can increase or decrease this when you see certain keyword strings working and others falling off. I highly recommend watching your AMS ads carefully. You aren't going to go broke doing ads unless your daily budget is too high, but I do see a lot of fluctuation in ad results. I recommend watching them and adjusting your bids when you see particular words giving you more traction.

As I mentioned previously, impressions matter, but so does cost per click. Ideally, you want high impressions with a low CPC. What's low? It depends a lot on your market segment, of course, and the strength of your keyword strings. I love seeing the ACOS (average cost of sales) somewhere around 30-57%, but this will also depend on whether your book is in Kindle Unlimited, because the AMS ad system doesn't count page reads, it counts sales. So you might have a very solid ACOS with a book that's in Kindle Unlimited, but if you're selling books *and* your page reads have gone up, the ads are likely doing well for you.

Amazon now also offers suggested bids, which I also find quite helpful, and I'll often use their suggested bids for any and all keyword strings I add provided that the number isn't too high. For example, for some books I've worked on, the suggested bid is $2 a click. With a $10 a day max budget, this will eat through your marketing dollars pretty quickly. So be selective when higher bid recommendations are suggested.

PROFITABILITY OF YOUR KEYWORD STRINGS

Sometimes keyword strings will start off strong and then drop off. When that happens, I recommend raising your bid on that keyword and see what happens. It may be that the bid isn't sufficient to keep pulling in readers. The other reason for the drop-off could be because the interest in the topic has subsided. I see this a lot with trendy topics and keyword strings that mirror the newsy, pop culture, or seasonally-focused books.

By the same token, if you see a keyword that's getting clicks but no tangible sales, I'd pause it, because it means you're wasting your money.

BOOSTING YOUR AMS CAMPAIGNS

In testing I've done, I've found that for genre fiction books in particular, doing ads on books that aren't part of the Kindle Unlimited program don't work as well as the books in KDP Select, which are always part of this program. Why? Because a lot of fiction readers in Kindle Unlimited are getting book recommendations from these ads, and although you may not see it in direct book sales, you'll definitely see it in page reads in Kindle Unlimited.

Books in a series, or which include multiple books about a theme, also tend to increase your overall sales. For example, let's say you write about saving money, starting a business, or parenting. Having multiple books out, even if you're only running ads for one of them, will help with your overall exposure, and potentially increase book sales for other books because you're attracting more readers

Another way to boost your Amazon ads is by adding the ad keyword strings to your book page, either via your book description, or any enhanced content you can include via Amazon Author Central. If you can include a keyword or two in your subtitle, even better. Keep in mind that your Amazon page is spidered, much like your website is spidered by Google, for example. Having ad keyword strings there is not only a great idea, but it's mandatory if you want to get good bounce from your ads.

FINDING GREAT KEYWORD STRINGS FOR YOUR AMAZON ADS

For Amazon ads to be successful, you must find the right keyword strings. Of all the things you do related to setting up your ads, this will take you the most time. The good news is, once you find some good keyword strings, you can probably keep running them for as long as you want to run your ads.

Amazon caps your keyword strings at 1,000 – though to start with I'd recommend looking for 300 to 400 keywords/keyword strings. I know this seems like a lot, but there are some easy ways and fun shortcuts for collecting them that I'll share with you later in this book.

Finding keyword strings isn't as hard as you might think. If you've gotten this far in the book and read the chapters about Amazon keyword strings, you know I like to talk a lot about supply and demand: Meaning high demand, low supply.

One of the biggest problems authors face when choosing keyword strings for their book page, or their Amazon ads, is when they choose words that have very little search momentum or, conversely, are far too competitive. Like "contemporary romance" for a romance novel.

The other thing to consider is the *how*, as in how your consumer searches, and, as we've discussed, consumers search based on their needs. If you have a book about gluten intolerance, your consumer may search for "wheat allergies," because they're coming at this from their pain points, not yours. For the purposes of breaking this down in a way that's easy to implement, I'm going to break down this chapter by keyword strings for fiction vs. keyword strings for nonfiction.

UNDERSTANDING THE DIFFERENT KEYWORD MATCH TYPES

Last year Amazon started expanding what it offered in terms of match types for keywords. Right now they offer broad, phrase, and exact keyword matches. So let's look at what this means and why it matters.

Match types will pull in different audiences, so it's important to understand the distinction before you jump into adding your keyword strings. But there's a shortcut around this as well that I'll show you in a minute. For now, let's see what each of them means:

Broad Match Search: this is the most flexible of keyword match types, allowing your keyword to show up in a variety of forms. For example, let's say your keyword is Star Wars. Your ad could show up for searches including: Star Wars Movie, Star Wars Book, Star Wars T-shirt. Conversely, it could also show up for movie Star Wars, book Star Wars, and so on. Broad gives you a lot of flexibility, but it's also a bit like casting a very wide net, which may work in some instances, but it could also start adding up in terms of paying for clicks on keyword terms that aren't related to you at all. An example of this would be using "Star Wars T-shirt" if all you have to offer is a book.

Phrase Match Search: is a bit less flexible, but also broad enough to pull in a good number of searches. Phrase match allows you to narrow your search terms using specific phrases. The key feature with this particular match type is that it allows you to control the word order. This helps to eliminate searches where a reader inserts a word (like the term "used") in between your keyword strings. However, it will include words before or after your keyword phrase. So while it's similar to broad match, it still keeps it within your target market. Meaning that if you have keyword strings like "Star Wars book" it won't show for T-shirts, mouse pads, or any other Star Wars paraphernalia.

Exact Match Search: this is the most limited of all search terms, and while this may seem like a bad thing, there are phrases that certainly can work well within the parameters of specific words which I'll discuss in a moment. But you should know that using exact match will limit your options, and that's okay if it's what you're trying to accomplish. For example, using Star Wars books will bring up searches for Star Wars book, but not book Star Wars.

WHICH MATCH TYPE IS RIGHT FOR YOUR AD CAMPAIGN?

The short answer is: it depends. The long answer is a bit more involved and, frankly, in nearly all the ads that I run, I will often add the keyword strings and experiment with different match types. Meaning I'll add in each set of keyword strings and then isolate each by Phrase, Exact, and Broad match. That way I can see which keyword strings do better in terms of each match type.

In certain other cases, such as with author names, you may not want to use broad match, because if the author has too much "other" stuff, like a non-book product, you could wind up in too many non-relevant searches.

AUTHOR NAMES AND BOOK TITLES AS KEYWORD STRINGS

This is still a recommended strategy, though I tend to use it more often for fiction than nonfiction. If you're going to do this, stay away from broad match and stick with phrase or exact, otherwise you'll pull up too much "other" stuff, depending on the book title you're aligning with.

You can also use your name in the keyword strings, too. However, match types will vary depending on whether you're fiction or nonfiction. I recommend using exact match for fiction, and phrase or broad match for nonfiction.

NEGATIVE KEYWORD STRINGS

Using negative keyword strings in the right way is another great opportunity to narrow your searches and not spend money on ads that aren't working for you. Keyword strings you want to rank as negative should be used carefully, because you don't want to omit searches that could be great for your sales.

What I'd recommend is starting with the term "used" (unless you're selling used books) and keeping an eye on your dashboard to see what's pulling in traffic and what's wasting money. You can then alter your keyword strings, stopping them altogether or adding particular phrases to the negative bin, which will prevent these searches from dinging your daily budget!

FINDING YOUR KEYWORD STRINGS

In the following section I'm going to divide up search protocol by fiction and nonfiction, because these two keyword searches are vastly different from what they used to be. First, we'll look at finding nonfiction keyword strings to match your sales objectives.

KEYWORD STRINGS FOR NONFICTION

Amazon's new ad system radically changed how we search for nonfiction keyword strings, and it's become much more aligned with Google searches, meaning that in large part you can use Google to find your keyword strings. If you've ever run a Google ad campaign, you're probably already familiar with their Keyword Planner tool, but if you're not, it's very easy to use. You need to log into your Google account to access it, and if you're already running Google ads you can just search for the keyword planner tool. If you've never run ads via Google, just set up a quick (and free) account to get access to it.

One thing I like to do when I'm searching for keyword strings for Amazon is dig into the needs of the readers searching. Earlier in this book I described finding keyword strings for an Amazon optimization I did for a book on Lyme disease, and earlier I discussed how the reader is searching for the problem, not the disease itself.

The same is true for your ads. Though Lyme disease will most definitely be part of your keyword strings, you'll also want to add the reader "pain points" to your list. Meaning: what's bringing them to your book. If you don't know this, you can play around with the Google Keyword Planner and find out. Some searches will net you tons of results while others may only give you two or three keyword strings, so you'll definitely want to play around, maybe adding the term "book" to your keyword strings. For example, I was searching for keyword strings related to WWII and found that it helped narrow down the searches considerably when I added the term "book" to the keyword strings.

Here's an example of one search I ran for my own book:

You'll see that Google ranks these as High, Medium, and Low, describing the search volume within Google, and I've found it closely mirrors the Amazon searches as well. In this case, the search turned up over one thousand keyword strings, so I grabbed the top five hundred with high and medium volume.

AMAZON'S KEYWORD SUGGESTIONS FOR NONFICTION

Previous versions of the AMS dashboard have offered an unimpressive list of keyword suggestions, but that's no longer the case. Here's an example of what the dashboard suggested for my ad:

Many of these were good enough to add, so I did.

USING AUTHOR NAMES AND BOOK TITLES

This is no longer mandatory for nonfiction, but if you're running short on keyword strings, or if the ones you pulled up in Google's Keyword Planner aren't great, you can certainly add in author book titles that are similar to yours. You'll want to follow the instructions for Fiction in order to do this. Just keep in mind that readers are looking for a solution, so be sure to align yourself with books that offer that.

KEYWORD STRINGS FOR GENRE FICTION

Genre fiction always seems more aligned with other authors and book titles, so let's start there. There's an easy way to grab authors, and that's by going to your Author Central Page on Amazon and start pulling up similar authors there. Here's an example of an author page from one of our authors, and you can see under the Also Bought section that there's a pre-populated list to get us started:

Basically, what I'm going to do is start with these authors, using their names and book titles, and start building my keyword strings list. Just click on any author, and it'll pull up their page and list of their books. Then start taking notes!

I may also go to the list of also-bought on these author pages, too, and keep building until I'm satisfied with the number of keyword strings I have.

KEYWORD STRINGS FOR MEMOIRS, LITERARY FICTION, WOMEN'S FICTION

These keyword strings will fall into the same bucket as mentioned above, except you might be more inclined to pull in keyword strings readers are using in their searches. For example, in the case of a memoir about Alzheimer's you might use that in your keyword, and so on.

CHILDREN'S FICTION, YOUNG ADULT FICTION

Much like the above, your keyword strings for children's books and young adult may fall more heavily into the blend of author titles and solutions. For example, a children's book on kindness might benefit from the keyword string: teaching children kindness.

USING THE GOOGLE KEYWORD PLANNER FOR FICTION

As I mentioned, you can certainly use the Google keyword planner, but the results will most definitely be more mixed than they are for nonfiction. You could also use keyword strings you find on Amazon, such as "romance and mystery book," and so on. Let's discuss how to do that:

USING AMAZON'S INTUITIVE SEARCH TO FIND KEYWORD STRINGS FOR FICTION

The first step in this process is choosing the phrases and search terms. I recommend that you start with a list of existing search terms your readers might input into the Amazon search bar to get to the books they're looking for. You probably developed a comprehensive list when you worked your way through the How to Research Keyword Strings chapter and already know which ones best resonate with your readers. You'll want to keep your earlier list handy for this exercise, although your ultimate goal is a bit different this time.

With the help of Amazon's intuitive search, you'll start to pull up keyword suggestions while you type in your keyword strings. Let's say you have a paranormal time travel romance. You could start by typing in the word, "paranormal." When you do, you'll see this box pop up. Take note of the search phrases that pop up and jot them down. This is the first series of keyword strings you'll want to use. However, keep in mind that you'll only want to use relevant keyword strings. If your book isn't a paranormal gay romance, you won't want to include that term.

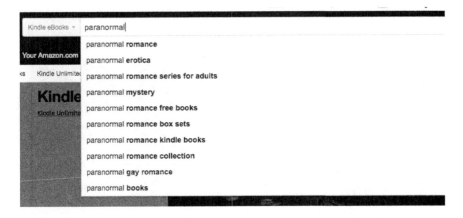

Another way to search is to pop in your keyword and the term "and," or start digging through the alphabet. For example, you can type in, "Romance a," "b," "c," and so on through the alphabet. Remember that Amazon is showing you these because people have searched using them, so going through the alphabet like this could help you find keyword strings you haven't thought of.

Note: You can do this for fiction and nonfiction to help expand your reach.

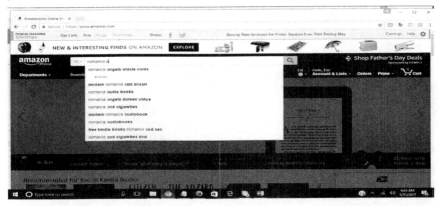

For fiction, in most every case, readers will search based on book type. Use categories like "mystery thriller," "sci-fi fantasy," or "paranormal romance."

But for nonfiction, consumers will always search for something to meet or help them better understand their specific need. Let's say you have a book about small business, growing the business, or creative ways to get your business started. You may start by typing "small business" into the search bar. As soon as you do, this intuitive search starts to populate:

Once you've done this and collected a good number of keyword strings, it's time for…

ONE FINAL NOTE ON KEYWORD STRINGS

When you include book titles, I recommend staying away from one-word titles. I haven't personally achieved a good CPC (cost per click) by using them. For example: "Hot," or "Smokin'," which you tend to see a lot in romance, are probably too broad and won't get you a good kickback in search. Or worse, it'll cost you a lot of money and yield very little in sales.

I recommend starting with 300-400 keyword strings. However, keep in mind that you can pair these by using the different search matches (broad, phrase, and exact)—thereby increasing the number of keyword strings you have in each campaign.

ADDING KEYWORD STRINGS TO YOUR ADS

The last and final step is adding your keyword strings to your ad. You'll want to add them manually since uploading an Excel file never seems to work. While you do this, you may see other recommended keyword strings pop up in the keyword ad box. Feel free to add as many of those as you feel are appropriate:

Suggested ⓘ   **Enter keywords**   Upload file

Match type ⓘ

Exact ⧉

nancy herkness
nicole deese
nicole elliot
nicole morgan
nora roberts
piper sullivan
raeanne thayne
rebecca boxall
richard paul evans
robyn carr

piper sullivan kindle books
piper sullivan kiss me love me
piper sullivan stranded
piper sullivan books
piper sullivan free kindle
piper sullivan accidentally
piper sullivan small town protectors
piper sullivan accidentally wifed
piper sullivan dating the doctor
piper sullivan accidental marriage

Select all keywords

WRITING A GREAT BOOK AD

If you've ever done Google Ads, Facebook ads, or Twitter, you already know you don't get a lot of room to work with in terms of ad content, so keep it short and sweet.

Statistics like percentages, and numbers like "top 5," are great attention grabbers, so if you can find a way to work them in, and they make sense for your topic, do it.

I also find it helps to link the ad content to keyword strings you plan to use if and when at all possible. By linking keyword strings to ads, you're also giving them the best chance to be seen, since the keyword strings match those in the ad.

For example, I linked an ad together with keyword strings like, "book marketing," "book promotion," and "book success," and the ad had the same keyword strings in it. Essentially, what happens when you do this, is Google sees the ad with all the keyword strings supporting it and gives it more visibility because there's more of a match.

If you are truly stuck for books, authors, and keyword strings, and barely made it to 200 or 300, you may be stuck and unable to do a variety of ads. But that's okay. This isn't a deal-breaker. Your ads will still work well enough to make this worth your while.

FURTHER CUSTOMIZING YOUR ADS

However, if you wind up with a ton of keyword strings, or you want to explore more areas, let's take a minute to discuss customizing ads to specific topics, specialties, or areas of focus.

Let's say your book fits under a few areas, which most books do. For example, you might have a book about growing a new business, gluten intolerance, food allergies, or even a genre fiction book. Each of these titles has a subset of interest that you probably found in your book research.

For the small business book, you might have found strings of keywords that talked about the importance of promoting your business in social media, and maybe even found a whole bunch of great social media books. Or maybe there's a chapter or two in your book about business accounting, and you found a whole slew of books about setting up accounting procedures if you're in a new business. Each of these areas of focus likely brought up a whole number of keyword strings, as well as book titles and authors. I would recommend grouping some of your ads to serve a particular market segment if you have enough keyword strings and a big enough ad budget to do so.

What you'll do next, to use the business book example, is use words like "social media," if you're tying into your string of social media and marketing books. Or "simple accounting," if you're after business owners who need to focus on this. Make sense?

WRITING YOUR AD

If you're doing ads based on keyword strings, you'll want to include some of the keyword strings in the ad itself. If you aren't, and you are not sure where to start, do a search on Amazon in your genre, niche, or subject, and see what kinds of Sponsored Posts get your attention. The ads are all pretty short in terms of word count, so you don't have a lot of room to work with anyway.

Something I've also done is create two identical campaigns using the same keyword strings, only with different ads, especially different ad copy, to see which gets a greater number of impressions. Keep in mind that 1,000 impressions means it was shown to 1,000 customers.

PRACTICE MAKES PERFECT

I know this is a lot to consider, and sounds like a lot of work, so I want to encourage you to test different strategies. Maybe try a couple of ads using statistics or numbers, and then try a couple of ads using keyword strings. If you have more than one buyer market, you should test ads that use specific sales angles for those markets.

Nothing is always going to work across the board, but you will learn a lot more from testing different approaches than you will by spending all your ad budget on a single ad.

FUN AMAZON HACKS

AMAZON AUTHOR CENTRAL

Every Amazon author, regardless of when or what they've published, has an author page which shows up along with your books when you search for the author name on Amazon—if you've claimed your pages.

Many authors have not claimed their pages, however. If you're not sure whether you've claimed yours yet, head on over to www.authorcentral. amazon.com/. You can access it using your Amazon sign-in. Keep in mind that even if you are traditionally published, you can still have an Amazon author page.

In order to claim the page, you must sign in and add content to the page. First, make sure all your books are claimed under your author page. It's easy enough—simply list them in Author Central by inserting their ISBNs and posting them to your page. Amazon will double-check your entries for accuracy. Once they do, you'll find a library of your books on your Author Central page.

In addition to your Amazon US page, you should also check out your international pages, which I'll cover in a minute!

Take a look at this standard Amazon author page:

As you can see, this author has added her bio, listed her books, and has book detail pages, which we'll discuss shortly. This works for both print and eBooks—basically, any book you have on Amazon can be added to your Amazon author page via Author Central. Also, notice you can program your author page to show your recent tweets and blog posts. And there's an option for your readers to follow your author page, which means they'll get announcements every time you publish a new book.

FARMING DATA FROM AMAZON AUTHOR CENTRAL

One of the bigger benefits of accessing your Author Central page is the data. An author can now get lots of data about their pages, like sales numbers—both Nielsen BookScan and Amazon data.

If you aren't familiar with Nielsen BookScan, it's the gold standard by which all your print sales are judged. Unlike Amazon sales numbers, which aren't made public, anyone with a BookScan account can access your sales data. You can also see all your reviews across all your books. Here's a snapshot of what this dashboard looks like currently.

If you click on "sales info" that takes you to the sales data, and this information is invaluable. Keep in mind that the data on this dashboard only refers to Amazon sales. If your publisher has a subscription to Nielsen BookScan independently, they can view data across all sales channels, including bookstores, Target, and Walmart, if the book is being sold there. The Amazon sales data is strictly for their site.

You can also check your author rank, which may show up on some book pages. Unlike BookScan data, your Author Rank takes into consideration your eBook and print sales, across all of Amazon and also within your genre, so Amazon will let you scroll down and see the breakdown specific to your market.

ADDING REVIEWS TO YOUR BOOK PAGE VIA AUTHOR CENTRAL

Dressing up your Amazon book page is a high priority for authors. Previously we were at the mercy of whoever reviewed the book on Amazon and whatever details the publisher decided to add.

Not anymore. Now you can go in and add reviews *you* choose to help dress up the page. Here's how: Once your books are listed on your page, meaning you've connected them to your account, just click on the book title, and it will open to a page that lets you fill in all the back-end detail. It's that easy. You can do the same with endorsements.

Also, the editing in Amazon is pretty sophisticated, so be sure to bold and underline portions of your reviews, like headlines and names, whenever possible. It works like Word, and makes it easy to draw the eye to a particular sentence or section of the review. If you want to know more about how to dress it up, just go back to the chapter **How Great Amazon Book Descriptions Help Indie Authors Sell More Books**, which gives you step-by-step instructions.

You'll notice that you can also add a book description to your Author Page. I don't know if it's something traditional authors have access to, but I will caution you that this part of Author Central is a bit glitchy. It does not allow you to use more than 480 words.

And beware! Once you update it on Author Central, unfortunately, you can't go back and change it. *Ever.* If you want a description longer than 480 words, you should reconsider updating your book description here. Here's the notice posted in the book description section:

Important: Once you make a change to a section here, your publisher will not be able to make any further changes to the same section. If you are a Kindle Direct Publishing author, and you make changes to your Product Description here, you will no longer be able to make edits via KDP.

> ## Monitoring Reviews on Amazon
>
> You can monitor your reviews on Amazon from your Author Central page. A word to the wise: Thank people for their reviews. It's a great way to spread the love and network with readers and reviewers. But this isn't the place to enter into detailed discussion. A simple thank-you is your best bet. We'll cover more about reviews later in this book.

FOLLOW AUTHOR FEATURE

Recently Amazon enhanced the author/reader experience by adding a yellow "Follow" bar to the Author Central page, right under your author photo:

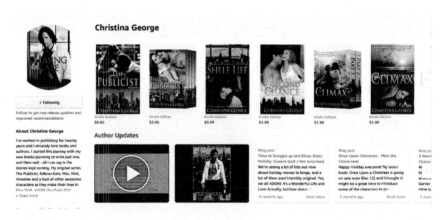

Encourage your readers to follow you. When they do, they'll automatically be notified whenever you publish a new book or set up a pre-order.

ENHANCING YOUR AMAZON HEADLINE

In addition to farming data, adding reviews and monitoring them, and using the "follow" feature, you can add some style-enhancers to your headline when you upload your book through the Amazon dashboard. Keep in mind that you can't make these changes through Author Central; it all has to be done from the dashboard. Although this won't affect your algorithm per se, it will help make your book description more visually appealing.

It's the difference between this:

Book Description
Publication Date: **May 18, 2011**

Can low profile, not-yet-famous authors get published and sell significant numbers of books? These authors say "Yes!" and tell how.

"...a comprehensive guide to marketing a book...[a] well-written, engaging resource that's loaded with specific tips.... Brimming with creative ideas, Sell More Books! :

- ForeWord Reviews

Writers and publishers will find the latest insider tips on writing and publishing more marketable books. Learn up-to-date information on publishing options, social net

Includes hundreds (300+ pages in print) of practical book-selling strategies for both traditionally and self-published authors. Learn which methods may work best for waste of time.

And this:

Book Description
Publication Date: **December 3, 2013**

If you're ready to sell more books on Amazon, you must read this one now.

UPDATED as of December 3, 2013 with new information!

Do you know that Amazon has a secret algorithm, and if you trigger it, they will actually help you sell books?

This easy-to-use guide will walk you through step-by-step what you need to do to kick Amazon's algorithm into high gear.

This book is a **MUST** for any author looking to get more sales and more exposure on Amazon!

Here are some of the headline enhancers available:
- Bolding: The text you want bolded
- Italics: <i>The text you want italicized</i>
- Headline: <h1>The text you want for a headline</h1>
- Amazon Orange Headline: <h2>The text you want bolded in orange</h2>

You can add in numbered lists and bullet points, too.

ANOTHER BOOST FOR YOUR BOOKS

Within the Author Central dashboard is a very underused, little-known area that can really help enhance your books. It's called "Editorial Reviews," and I think it is overlooked a lot because the name is a bit misleading. The space can be used for more than just reviews. You can use it to add many, fun, informative enhancements to your Author Central page. First, let's look at where to find the page. When you're in your Author Central dashboard, click on Books.

Once you click on a book, you'll see this under Editorial Reviews:

Review Add
Empty

Product Description Edit
Packed with Romance and Sex, here's what readers are saying about The Publicist Series:

"...this book grabbed my interest from page one. I'm sure Ms. George has more than a few industry insiders chuckling at her stories and cringing at how close to home they hit.
Scandalicious Book Reviews of Romance Books

"If you're looking for this year's Fifty Shades of Grey, you've found it with The Publicist." JollyBuzz

What happens when you fall in love with a man you can never have?

Vivienne has it all, a successful writing career, a hit movie, a life most women dream of. The only thing missing is someone to share it with. So when a handsome, successful doctor saves her from near death, Vivienne is certain she's finally met the man of her dreams... Until she discovers who he is... or rather who his father is. The man who single-handedly tore apart her brother's life. Can she put the past behind her? Will she choose family over love? Or will she lose the man she feels destined to be with?

I read the first book which was brilliant! So I was very excited when the second book came out. This one was better than the first! It pushed the limits with the steamy scenes in the bedroom and the affair that Kate and Mac had. Always, in an affair there will be obstacles to get past. Some of the things that happen in the book makes me wonder how accurate the description of the publishers job is. I'm assuming it's pretty accurate. Kate finds herself growing and becoming more focused on herself so she can make a difference in her field, which any one would do in her shoes. I really felt book one was great but this one blew it out of the water! Great book! ZootZoot · Reader review in romance and sex category!

From the Author Add
Empty

From the Inside Flap Add
Empty

From the Back Cover Add
Empty

About the Author Add
Empty

Now you can add all sorts of fun stuff to this page. What kinds of things can you add? You can develop your "dream" Q&A as a great way to share all the information you wish the media or readers would ask, or as a smart way to work in a bunch of information that just couldn't fit into your book description.

A personal note from the author is a clever way to drive home why you're passionate about your subject or genre.

Or include information about a contest you're running, or a mention of your social media, website, and more.

I've seen some authors use this space to update their readers about other promotions they're doing, too. For example, when you run discounted promotions or a freebie, mention it here. Amazon says it takes up to 72 hours to update, but I've never had it take that long. Still, plan ahead, because if the Amazon machine gets busy and the update you're making happens in a limited timeframe, you'll want to plan ahead.

ADDING EVENTS TO YOUR AUTHOR PAGE

Another fun way to enhance your Author Page on Amazon is using the events feature. I've noticed that a lot of authors aren't using it, and that's a shame, because it's a nice way to help add some content to your page and spread the word about your upcoming events. While the events are limited to in-person events, like speaking engagements or book signings, you can also list online events by connecting the webinar, or whatever it is you're doing, to the venue.

For example, in the screen shot below you'll see the first event, from May 27 was for IBPA. In order to list that event in the Amazon calendar, I linked it to IBPA's office address. That's all you need to do! If you're doing an online event connected to a company (or for yourself), link it to the business address. Of course it goes without saying that you'll want to keep privacy in mind. If the business address is a home address, link it instead to a post office box whenever possible.

Author's Upcoming Events

Date	City, State	Venue	Event
Mar 27, 2019 10:00 AM	Manhattan Beach, CA	Independent Book Publishers Association	Mastering Amazon: Ads, Leveraging Your List, and Mastering Amazon Ads! (this event is online!) See details
May 6, 2019 2:00 PM	NEW YORK, NY	The New York Marriott Downtown	ASJA Writer's Conference See details
Jul 26, 2019 10:00 AM	New York, New York	Marriott Marquis Times Square	Romance Writers of America - National Conference See details

You can access the events at the bottom of the Author Page. Just click on "add event" and you're set!

Author Page

Content you provide will appear on Amazon's Penny C. Sansevieri Page after a short delay.
> Visit Amazon's Penny C. Sansevieri Page

Biography   edit biography   delete

Penny C. Sansevieri, Founder and CEO Author Marketing Experts, Inc., is a best-selling author and internationally recognized book marketing and media relations expert. She is an Adjunct Professor teaching Self-Publishing for NYU.

Her company is one of the leaders in the publishing industry and has developed some of the most innovative Social Media/Internet book marketing campaigns. She is the author of sixteen books, including How to Sell Your Books by the Truckload on Amazon, 5 Minute Book Marketing, and Red Hot Internet Publicity, which has been called the "leading guide to everything Internet."

AME has had dozens of books top bestseller lists, including those of the New York Times, USA Today, and Wall Street Journal.

To learn more about Penny's books or her promotional services, you can visit her web site at www.amarketingexpert.com.

Blogs   add blog

Blog Feed	Status
http://www.amarketingexpert.com/feed/	New posts will appear on the Author Page within 24 hours of posting. Learn More

Events   add event

Date	City, State	Venue	Event	
May 6, 2019 2:00 PM	NEW YORK, NY	The New York Marriott Downtown	ASJA Writer's Conference	
Jul 26, 2019 10:00 AM	New York, New York	Marriott Marquis Times Square	Romance Writers of America - National Co...	

THE MOST OVERLOOKED AMAZON SALES TOOL: INTERNATIONAL AUTHOR CENTRAL PAGES!

Have you ever looked at your KDP sales dashboard and wondered how you can sell more books in other countries? We have a client who noticed she's selling a bunch of books in Japan and wondered if she could rack up more sales there.

In addition to pitching specific blogs in those areas, or doing advertising geared to that market, all of which requires time and money, you could also take a few minutes and claim your Author Central pages in these countries. It's quick and easy, and the best part is, all the international Author Central pages are the same.

First, here are the countries that do *not* have Author Central pages set up.

- Brazil
- Canada
- China
- Mexico
- Netherlands

These countries all list your book, but don't have a page connecting all your titles. The irony is most of our authors don't sell a lot of books in these areas unless the book relates to that country specifically. For example, a book about Mexican heritage might do well on Amazon's website in Mexico.

Next, let's look at the countries that do have Author Central pages:

- France
- Japan
- UK
- Germany

Here's a quick look at what you can expect to see on a few of these pages. First, France:

It is slightly different from your US Amazon Author Central page, and, of course, in a different language, right? Naturally your author bio will remain in English, but if your books are in English, too, this works just fine. Next, let's take a look at Germany:

The German version of Amazon Author Central looks more like the version you're used to seeing, but once again in a different language.

A note regarding Japan's Author Central pages: First, you have to register yourself there. Just use the same username and password you use for the US site, and it takes just a few clicks. Don't let the "new registration" deter you.

From there, the system will ask to verify your e-mail. In fact, all the sites do this. Once your e-mail is verified, you're good to go.

YOUR AUTHOR CENTRAL TOOLS

When you're doing this, use the Chrome browser. It has a quick "translate" button, which is far more accurate than any others I've tried. It takes one quick step to translate a Japanese website into English. And English to Japanese.

First, you'll need your bio. You can use whatever bio you created for yourself on your US page, but it might be nice if you adjust it to suit the country you're targeting. For example, let's say you have an international mystery that takes the reader from the UK to Germany and beyond. You might want to address that in your bio, and the international connection could help pull in a reader from the countries mentioned.

IMAGES AND VIDEO

A while back Amazon removed the ability to "add images" to the actual book page but has now moved it to the Author Central Page. You can add up to eight images, and the best part is that you can replace them with new images all the time. You've released a new book? Add a new image. Or if you have a promotion coming up, or you've won an award, then by all means add an image of the award, too. Readers love learning about your awards!

Your video can be anything from you talking at an event to an actual book video/trailer. Video is a great enhancement tool. And the best part? You can upload as many as you'd like. I've done as many as three or four.

YOUR BOOKS

The other fun piece about this is that the system is very good at grabbing all your books. Just make sure that you click on the "Books" tab.

THE FINAL RESULT!

Here you can check out Author Central Pages across several countries. They're robust, engaging, and keep all the author's books in one place so the readers can find them easily.

- France: www.amazon.fr/-/e/B00AB0CHJQ
- Germany: www.amazon.de/-/e/B00AB0CHJQ
- Japan: www.amazon.co.jp/-/e/B00AB0CHJQ
- UK: www.amazon.co.uk/-/e/B00AB0CHJQ

HOW TO ACCESS THESE PAGES

And to make it simple for you, here are the links to access and update each of your pages. Yes, it's that easy!

- France: www.authorcentral.amazon.fr/
- Germany: www.authorcentral.amazon.de/gp/home
- Japan: www.authorcentral.amazon.co.jp/gp/home
- UK: www.authorcentral.amazon.co.uk/gp/home

BUT DOES IT SELL BOOKS?

Yes, I can tell you it does. In fact, authors we've done this for have seen a substantial uptick in international market sales when they updated these pages. Keep in mind that if you're already selling books in these markets, this will help you a great deal. If you aren't selling books in, let's say, Germany, you might not see any immediate effect there. But it's still a fabulous thing to have, update, and optimize!

AMAZON X-RAY

A while back Amazon quietly released a new service within its Kindle program called X-Ray, and basically it's a way to provide additional or enhanced content to your readers via their Kindle devices. And because Amazon doesn't advertise it, most authors and readers overlook it. But if you take the time to play around with it, you'll find it's a pretty fun tool to use.

Here is Amazon's description of what the X-Ray feature is:

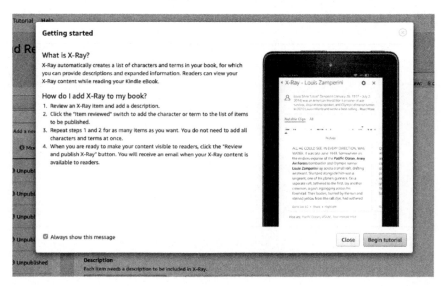

First off, you'll want to get access to the X-Ray feature on your KDP dashboard. If you click the three dots next to your book, it'll pop up as an option:

When you click that link, it'll take you to the back-end X-Ray dashboard like this:

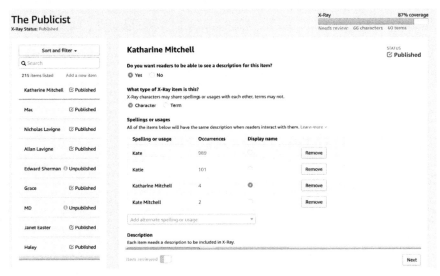

And you'll notice that down the left-hand side, most of the character names have "published" beside them, which means that content has been published under that character name. Now this could have been because the author did this already, but sometimes it's not. Sometimes Amazon grabs something random (as you'll see in the screenshot below) while other times it grabs the Wikipedia description. In my case, they grabbed the description for a penny because of my name—which didn't at all fit the content.

Each item needs a description to be included in X-Ray.

| Write a custom description ✏ | OR | Choose a Wikipedia article W |

Custom descriptions are **highly recommended**.

(i) X-Ray automatically chose this text from the book as a description. To replace it, write a custom description or select a Wikipedia article.

Janet was a sure thing.

Source: **Excerpt**

Leaving the description "Janet was a sure thing" isn't helpful to this feature, and also means something entirely different from what was likely intended.

First and foremost, I suggest that you go through your books and check the X-Ray content. Once you publish it, readers can access it on their Kindle devices or tablets. Which means that they can access the X-Ray link in their tablet by clicking the icon, like this:

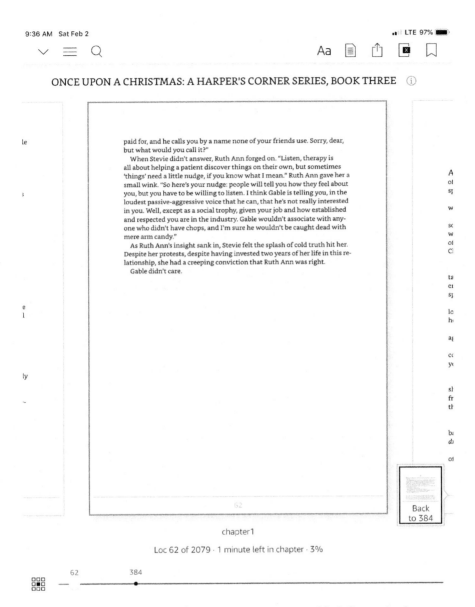

paid for, and he calls you by a name none of your friends use. Sorry, dear, but what would you call it?"

When Stevie didn't answer, Ruth Ann forged on. "Listen, therapy is all about helping a patient discover things on their own, but sometimes 'things' need a little nudge, if you know what I mean." Ruth Ann gave her a small wink. "So here's your nudge: people will tell you how they feel about you, but you have to be willing to listen. I think Gable is telling you, in the loudest passive-aggressive voice that he can, that he's not really interested in you. Well, except as a social trophy, given your job and how established and respected you are in the industry. Gable wouldn't associate with anyone who didn't have chops, and I'm sure he wouldn't be caught dead with mere arm candy."

As Ruth Ann's insight sank in, Stevie felt the splash of cold truth hit her. Despite her protests, despite having invested two years of her life in this relationship, she had a creeping conviction that Ruth Ann was right.

Gable didn't care.

62

chapter1

Loc 62 of 2079 · 1 minute left in chapter · 3%

62   384

They'll be able to see whatever content you added for each character name or keyword. With enhanced content you'll be able to offer readers more insight into the keyword, the character, or the backstory for whatever it is you're sharing in your book.

"Magdalena "Maggie", often dubbed the "leader" of the Coven, is as vivacious as she is beautiful. She's the catalyst and everyone's best friend. Maggie's parents run a local Mexican bistro called El Pueblo Penqueno, serving high end, foodie-worthy Mexican cuisine. When she's not hanging with the Coven, Maggie can often be found helping her father introduce new seasonal new dishes, like their Plantain Taquitos and Ceviche Mixto."
Location 385

CHAPTER6   (1)

Stevie read **Maggie's** text and shot back a quick response. **Maggie** was part of "the coven"—an unofficial term for the group of women she'd grown up with—but they'd mostly lost touch when she moved to the city.
Location 385

CHAPTER7   (16)

Stevie gave her a little wave and saw the front door open again. **Maggie** and Jessica walked in together.
Location 410

"Stevie!!" **Maggie** yelled out above the crowd. Several heads turned. "It's good to see you, girl."
Location 411

"It's good to see you, girl." **Maggie** wrapped her in a hug, and when she let her go, Jessica took her place.
Location 412

"Let's go grab our table," **Maggie** bubbled, weaving her way through the crowd. The table was in the back, not exactly private, but also not in the thick of things.
Location 415

Maggie and Jessica followed suit. "Coffee, ladies!" Adelaide was right behind them, holding a carafe of coffee in one hand and a tray with creamer, sugar and several cups stacked in the other.
Location 417

"Over here, Char!" **Maggie** waved. There were hugs all around. "How's the spin studio, going Charlotte?"
Location 419

"I was just sleeping." **Maggie** laughed, pouring herself a cup of coffee. "I have food!"

It's a fun tool, and can be used not just to add backstory for characters, but to enhance any nonfiction content you may have.

For example, with my own books on book marketing, I went in there and added additional information to particular terms. This works extremely well if you don't want to take readers too far outside of what you're explaining, where enhanced explanations don't necessarily make sense within the text, or if you just want to update the content. In one of my other marketing books, I had a chapter where I mentioned CreateSpace, which has since been folded into KDP, so I added an enhancement piece and addressed the changes. This was great, because the book wasn't really due for an update, but I could get in there and make some additional changes on X-Ray to give the reader a better, more current experience.

LETTING READERS KNOW ABOUT X-RAY

You may be wondering, since Amazon isn't widely promoting this, why should you care about X-Ray? Well, if you don't care that Amazon may be plugging whatever content they deem necessary into your book, then don't bother with it.

But if you want to be sure your book is the best it can be, and that you have access to and control of your X-Ray content, then I suggest not only getting in there and updating it, but letting readers know to look for it. You could send out a newsletter to your readers, as well as sharing it on social media. If you plan to do this, you could also mention it in your book intro (this works probably best with nonfiction).

MAKING X-RAY CONTENT FUN

Aside from adding character backstory or enhancing/updating existing non-fiction content, you could also create a sort of Easter egg hunt for fun things you've included in your book that readers can find and perhaps win prizes.

You can also include links to other external content, too, like blog posts you'd like readers to see, etc. The links aren't live, so I'd create a fun, shorter link using a Bit.ly or some other shortening URL service. Bit.ly allows you to customize the link, which makes it easy for a reader to remember or jot down!

THE SECRET TRICK TO BOOSTING YOUR KEYWORD STRINGS

I've spent so much time in this book discussing keyword strings: how to find them and how to use them. I talked about keyword strings in your book description and subtitle, or even using keyword strings in your title.

But what happens if not all these pieces are an option? Will your book tank? Is there anything else you can do? Well, the answer is: no, it won't tank your book. But certainly having more keyword strings on your book page will help it considerably. So what can you do? How about an author interview?

This simple tool—a quick, interesting interview with you, the fabulous author, available on your Author Page via Author Central—is a great way to enhance your keyword usage and push in more words you may not have been able to include otherwise.

My suggestion for the interview is to keep it interesting enough so folks will want to read the book, because if you're just adding content to be able to shove in more keyword strings, it won't necessarily help to keep readers on your page.

Ask a few questions—maybe up to five—and then answer them in such a way that you can use some of your keyword strings. You can also add keyword strings to the questions themselves. Have a look at the following interview one of our authors did:

Editorial Reviews

From the Author
Get to Know Christina George!

If you weren't writing contemporary romance, what genre would you write?
Probably thrillers, because I love the concept of this fast-paced, edgy story that keeps you guessing. The problem with writing romance novels is that it's addicting. So while I've had great story ideas for thrillers, I never really do anything with them because romance is always my go-to. And anyone who knows me knows I'm a romantic at heart!

Of all of your characters, which ones seem the most real to you and why?
I would have to say Kate and Mac from my original Publicist series seem the most real. The reason is hard to explain, but I think at her core Kate is a lot like me, or who I'd like to be all the time. She's flawed but confident, she makes bad choices and owns up to them. I can 100% relate to that.
In terms of Mac... well, that's a bit of interesting backstory because I dated a "Mac" that the character was modeled after. It wasn't as perfect as this contemporary romance character, of course. But he's where I got the idea. No, we didn't stay together, which in the end was for the best. But in romance novels you've got to have a HEA (happily ever after).

You're being held hostage by the last show you watched, who is holding you captive?
Great question! I'm being held hostage by the folks in Grey's Anatomy, which is sort of fitting for this interview since the show often cycles around the relationships that live and die within the walls of that hospital.
Also, I'm still not over Shonda Rhimes killing off Derek.

If you had to pick, where would you rather write? Noisy coffee shop or a quiet library, and why?
Coffee shop, without question. I love the noise element of it, which is odd - but I guess great for the creative juices. Also, there's always coffee at the ready. And snacks, a romance author has to have her snacks!

You're having a dinner party and can only invite five people - living or dead, who would they be?
Tom Petty for sure, and probably Prince so they could jam out. Princess Diana, without question. I'd invite ABBA (can they count as one person?) former President Eisenhower, and Amelia Earhart. Cool group, no?

Do you have any writing superstitions? Or funky/odd writing habits that you want to share with our readers?
I don't know about superstitions per se (though I'm not opposed to smudging my office after a particularly bad afternoon of writing), but I do create a book playlist on Spotify that I can listen to, while I'm writing. If I'm struggling with a particular character, I'll find a song for them and play it on repeat. I do that a lot, with a song on repeat, too. And not just a character song but a song that gets me into the vibe of writing contemporary romance.

What's a song that you hate people talking over?
Without question: Follow You, Follow Me by Genesis - it's from the 1970's and I simply adore it.

I had her post this under the Editorial Reviews section in the back end of Author Central and, voilá, more places to use keyword strings! It's a great, fun little tool to not only add some interesting content to your Amazon book page, but also use those keyword strings again and again!

10 SMART WAYS TO LAUNCH YOUR BOOK ON AMAZON

Creating an outstanding book launch is something every author aspires to do. However, for most of us the problem is that there's always a lot going on around the time you launch your book. Maybe you're planning a book launch party, some local signings, or even a big virtual event. But there are a few key elements specifically related to your Amazon launch that shouldn't be overlooked. With that in mind, let's dig into the Amazon ecosystem to better understand how books spike there during a book launch.

When you first launch your book on Amazon, there's some Amazon momentum that kicks in, almost organically, for any new release title. It can be short—very short in some cases—but quite powerful.

How long your new release Amazon boost lasts depends on a few things. Some of these you can control, but some you can't.

Genre, for example, makes a difference in how long your book sits in the new release category. The number of books launching at the same time (on the same day) as yours is also a factor. The third factor is algorithm, which is something you absolutely can control, and is easily woven into your book launch. The following steps don't require a huge effort, just a bit of planning ahead. If done right, they can pay big dividends in terms of the Amazon boost all new release titles get.

PRE-ORDER

I don't recommend this for all authors. If it's your first book, and you have no real platform, I'd skip it. Why? Because a pre-order is a great tool if you're ready to hit the ground running when your book launches. Meaning if you do a pre-order and launch your book, but it takes a month or months to get reviews, it can actually hurt your exposure on Amazon. The system is geared to pushing books that are selling right out of the gate. So if you decide to do a pre-order, don't do a long one. Two weeks or a month at the most, and be prepared to move quickly when you launch date arrives.

FREE BOOK TEASER

While this isn't a new release strategy per se, it's a great tool for boosting your overall book exposure. Here's how it works: Put the first few chapters of your book up as a free book edition. Meaning it's a permafree book sample with a link to your complete book. I've done it for mine, but the idea originally came from a David Baldacci title, which had a seven-chapter free preview to help boost the launch of his latest book. Have a look:

This isn't the first time Baldacci has done this, and frankly it's brilliant and really easy to do!

BOOK DESCRIPTION

Make sure your book description is sharp, focused, and impactful. Don't cram your entire description into one unreadable paragraph. Make sure your description has lots of white space, because remember: we scan, we don't read. And attention spans have shrunk from 20 minutes to an astonishing 8 seconds. So remember, you don't have a lot of time to get readers interested in your book. Lead with a strong headline, and don't bury your most important point at the bottom of the book description, because a reader may not get that far. And this is something to keep in mind for your existing titles as well as for any new book launches.

If you're interested to learn more about capturing attention spans, here's a piece on our blog!

SOCIAL PROOF

If your book is up for pre-order, you'll want to populate it with reviews quickly. And by quickly, I mean within the first week of the book going live. Sometimes authors complain that reviews get pulled when they go live too fast (meaning within 24 hours of the book launch), but I haven't seen that as a consistent problem. I've had books that have gone live and almost immediately start earning reviews. Rarely have they been pulled, but I know it does happen to a few authors, so proceed with caution. Because nothing can kill a book launch like having reviews appear and then disappear on Amazon!

BOOK AND EBOOK PRICING

Another element of a successful book launch is your pricing, and I recommend getting a bit creative with this. Generally I like to start a new book launch off with a slight price discount for the eBook or print book (though it's often easier to do this with the print book). Starting a book off at $2 below what the standard pricing will be is a good way to boost early exposure for the book. If you discount your eBook in particular, you could also boost it with eBook promos, which I'll address later on in this section.

AMAZON KEYWORD STRINGS & CATEGORIES

While this may seem counterintuitive, I'm going to suggest that you hold off doing keyword strings and categories right when the book launches on Amazon. Why? Because you gain a certain amount of momentum for a book while it's in the 'new release' arena. This can last for up to a month, as I mentioned previously.

What I'd suggest doing is adding keyword strings that include the term "new release romance" (or whatever your genre is) and then removing them after three weeks and adding in your final keyword strings, as well as adjusting your categories. I know a lot of authors who do this right at the launch, but I like holding off on that strategy until the momentum from the new release begins to diminish. This helps give the book another boost after the initial momentum starts to fade.

AMAZON ADS

I'd recommend starting Amazon ads at book launch if you can, and I'd suggest running these with "new release" in the body of the ad. You can change it once the book is "technically" no longer a new release. Readers like new and fresh, so take advantage of it by putting "new release" in your ads.

ALSO-BOUGHT

It's often tempting to send an email blast out to your family and friends to encourage them to buy your book. But this is a strategy you should proceed with cautiously, because often it will skew your Also Bought results if readers (who don't normally buy in your genre) click on your book. It can hurt, not help, your book launch algorithm. Let me explain.

The strip of also-boughts just under your book is populated from algorithms that directly relate to the person clicking on your book.

For example, let's say you've published a book about preserving classic cars and I'm on your mailing list, so you invite me to peruse it. I click the link to Amazon and bam! All my shopping history has now followed me to your book page. If I buy romance novels, or sci-fi, those shopping patterns will be reflected in your also-boughts. This matters, because it's how Amazon "learns" what category your book belongs in and, in turn, recommends your book under other author also-boughts to new readers. If the people clicking on your book aren't fans of your genre, that Also Bought strip will look confusing. By the same token, your book won't wind up in the also-boughts of books in your genre, because you've now taught the Amazon system that your classic car restoration book could also go under romance and sci-fi.

This algorithm will eventually fix itself, but in the first month or so, as tempting as it will be to invite friends and relatives to your Amazon page, if they aren't fans of the genre it could screw up your algorithm during this important book launch period. Consider waiting 30 days after you launch your book on Amazon to invite your friends and family to your page. That way the Also Bought area will have already populated with correct searches. Once your book is solid in the genre algorithm, it won't matter as much if someone outside their normal reading genre clicks on your book.

BOOK LAUNCH, EBOOK PROMOS

I love doing eBook promos, and it's especially fun to do them while your book isn't full price (yet), and you can still take advantage of the book launch sale you've got going. Plan to do at least one of these at the three-week mark of your book launch. This helps to keep the new release spike going too!

SPREADING OUT YOUR BOOK EDITIONS

One of the final options to extend the new release buzz is to separate out your release of editions of your book. For example, you may decide to release your eBook first, with your paperback, hardcover and audio following at later intervals. Each new edition of your book is a new book release, and spacing them out can help you gain new momentum each time a new edition launches on Amazon.

DOING FREE EBOOK PROMOTIONS

Promoting your book for free is great way to boost your exposure on Amazon and to help spark the algorithm. Know, however, that not all freebies are equal. By this I mean that it's more important to be strategic than to be fast.

UNDERSTANDING HOW FREEBIES WORK

One of the reasons I love KDP Select is because when you do a freebie on Amazon, the system pretty much takes care of it for you. All you have to do is set the dates and hit Schedule.

If you're not interested the Select program within KDP, you can do a freebie outside of Amazon. The Select system within KDP requires you to be on the Amazon site—exclusively—for ninety days. Some authors have a problem with that, though I never have. But eBook research has shown that Amazon continues to get the lion's share of sales in book and eBook sales. However, if you don't want to be exclusive, then KDP Select may not be for you.

For now, though, let's assume you're in the Select system. During the period your book is free, you'll see the sales rank rise. And even though it's in the free category, it's great, because you're gaining traction on Amazon and being seen by more potential readers.

When your book goes back to paid status, the book will flip to its original category again. It won't keep the sales rank you had when it was free, but it could still be fairly high, because most books continue to see a surge after you do the freebie.

TIMING YOUR FREEBIE

Ideally you should wait until the book has been up on the site for a while before you offer a freebie. I've found that waiting ninety days is best. You want to give it a chance to grow on its own. As I mentioned above, the book will flip from the paid category to the free one, and then back to paid once the giveaway is over. Although it ends up back where it started, it will grow because of residual momentum from the giveaway. In theory, the longer the book has been on Amazon, the stronger hold it has within the paid category and the faster you'll feel the boost when you do this promo.

PRICING AND REVIEW STRATEGIES

In addition to timing, pricing and reviewing are two aspects of eBook promotion that can make or break sales.

Generally I don't recommend starting any type of campaign like this without having *at least* eight to ten reviews on your page. With all the freebie specials being offered nowadays, most consumers won't go for a free book with a naked Amazon page (a page with no reviews).

Right after the freebie campaign you'll continue to see a lot of traffic on your page—the residual momentum you've created from the promotion. I've seen it last up to three days. If your book did well during the freebie period, this momentum will help it rise higher in the paid category, since the promotion helped trigger the internal Amazon algorithm.

The right pricing when it returns to the paid category will also help perpetuate this algorithm. If the book did well, it might be tempting to list it at a higher price. However, I recommend you keep your pricing low during the days immediately following your free promotion. How low? It depends on how your book was priced in the first place, but generally I suggest you discount it by half for just three days.

This may seem counterintuitive. I mean, you want to make money, right? What better way to sell tons of books at full price than by capturing the tsunami of traffic finding its way to your page because of your freebie?

You do want to make sales, but don't think short-term. Think long-term. If you can boost your book within a category with the right pricing, it will help to trigger a sales momentum you would never get otherwise. By keeping your book on your readers' radar screen by having it show up higher in the category, you'll have more sales long term.

EBOOK PROMOTION

Even if everyone loves free, you can't just put the book up on Amazon, mark it free, and call it a day. You have to promote it.

There are a lot of sites that let you list your book for free (see below). During your promotion, you should also be on sites like Twitter, sending messages, using hashtags, and pinging other accounts.

Here are websites and Twitter accounts I know would love to hear about your freebie, followed by a list of hashtag suggestions. Make sure you plan your freebie at least two weeks in advance, because sometimes listings on sites require that much notice. There are some paid listings, too. I've had good success with BookBub.com, Kindle National Daily, and Book Gorilla.

HERE'S A LIST OF FREE SITES WHERE YOU CAN LIST YOUR BOOK

www.katetilton.com/ultimate-list-sites-promote-free-ebook/
www.ereadernewstoday.com
www.pixelofink.com
www.indiesunlimited.com/freebie-friday
www.kindlenationdaily.com
www.kindlemojo.com
www.totallyfreestuff.com
www.icravefreebies.com/contact
www.kindleboards.com/free-book-promo/
www.indiebookoftheday.com/authors/free-on-kindle-listing/
www.ebooklister.net/submit.php
www.kindlebookpromos.luckycinda.com/?page_id=283
www.thedigitalinkspot.blogspot.com.es/p/contact-us.html
www.freekindlefiction.blogspot.co.uk/p/tell-us-about-free-books.html
www.freeebooksdaily.net/
www.freebookshub.com/authors/
www.frugal-freebies.com
www.ereaderiq.com/about/
www.askdavid.com/free-book-promotion
www.ebookshabit.com/about-us/
www.snickslist.com/books/place-ad/

www.awesomegang.com/submit-your-book
www.goodkindles.net/p/why-should-i-submit-my-book-here.html
www.kornerkonnection.com/index.html?fb=ebookkornerkafe
www.dailycheapreads.com
www.bookgoodies.com/authors-start-here/
www.indiebookoftheday.com
www.igniteyourbook.com/

TWITTER ACCOUNTS TO NOTIFY

@DigitalBkToday
@kindleebooks
@Kindlestuff
@KindlebookKing
@KindleFreeBook
@Freebookdude
@free
@free_kindle
@FreeReadFeed
@4FreeKindleBook
@FreeKindleStuff
@KindleUpdates
@Kindleebooks
@Kindlestuff
@Kindlemysbook
@Kindle_Freebies
@100freebooks
@kindletop100
@kindleowners
@IndAuthorSucess
@FreeEbooksDaily
@AwesometasticBk
@Bookyrnextread
@Kindle_promo
@KindleDaily
@Bookbub

HASHTAGS TO USE

#free
#freekindle
#freebook
#kindlepromo
#freeebook

Freebies are a great way to boost your overall exposure on Amazon, plus they can earn more reviews to help populate the page. I love doing freebies—I've often seen big sales bursts after a campaign has ended.

In addition to offering freebies, you can also promote your book with special pricing. Kindle Countdown Deals offers an opportunity to promote special pricing across a few days.

You pick the pricing, and you pick the days. Many of the free sites mentioned above will also let you promote your book if it's $0.99, which is another great way to get your book out there. Be aware, though, that the idea behind Kindle Countdown is to literally count down via your pricing. If you start the deal at $0.99, it goes up to $1.99 the next day, and so on until it's back at its regular price. We've found that too many different price points confuse the consumer. Pick one price, do Kindle Countdown, and just let it run for three to five days.

SUPPORTING YOUR PROMOTION WITH ADS

I always encourage authors to consider all the ways they can support their own work. Meaning, don't make one book promotion strategy fend for itself. If you're planning a freebie promotion, in addition to promoting it on sites that will list your book, or getting other accounts to Tweet about it, you should consider supporting it with ads.

And while Amazon ads and social media ads have their place, the platforms are pretty complex. If you know how to run those kinds of ads, definitely do it. But for those of you who are new to ads, or aren't comfortable enough with them yet, I have a solution: BookBub ads.

BookBub ads, unlike BookBub promotions, are available to all authors without restrictions, so you can bet you're already a sure thing.

They are also super easy to set up because BookBub has structured their ad creation to be relatively foolproof.

If your book is already in their system, you can search by ISBN or ASIN and they'll pull up your cover, give you a complimentary background to work with, and generate all your online retail links. If you're not in the system, you can simply manually upload a copy of your cover, add the retail links you want to focus on, and voilá.

Like most ads, the text for the ad content is minimal, so be smart and think of something truly mind-blowing—the cliff-hanger, the "must-have" feature, etc. And for the "buy now" button, this is where your discount comes into play. I suggest something super clear and timely like "FREE TODAY," with a plan to run the ad only for the days it's free.

Then you get to choose your genre(s), which is straightforward, as well as any authors you want to align yourself with. For this part I recommend going to the bestseller list on Amazon that you'd most want to join and start plugging the top author names into BookBub. BookBub will even show you how many of its followers are following that author to give you an idea of your reach if you include them.

Then set your budget and date range (I suggest cost-per-click) and you're finished. The nice thing is, cost-per-click won't blow through your budget unless people are genuinely interested.

The next-level move would be creating an ad leading up to your freebie. I do this for a lot of my clients because it creates some recognition for the author name, and definitely for the book cover.

Imagine a reader sees an ad for your book, and it encourages them to check it out on Amazon. Maybe they do check it out, but maybe they don't buy. That's not uncommon on the first try. But then they see an ad for your book the next week and it says "FREE TODAY"—the chances of them going back and downloading it are that much greater because they recognize your name, your book cover, and have previously checked out your book.

The old adage that it takes seven impressions with a product before someone buys is still pretty accurate, although we know for a fact that it's multiple, and this is how you play that game strategically.

ON TO THE NEXT PHASE...

I love discovering new opportunities for promotion on Amazon, and I'm always exploring new ways to get noticed. I hope you've enjoyed part one, and that the content benefits you in your Amazon book marketing enterprise.

Part two will look exclusively at book reviews and how to get more of them on Amazon—which is so important to your book's success. It will help you learn how to add more reviews and take your Amazon page to the next level.

Happy selling!

HOW TO GET REVIEWS BY THE TRUCKLOAD ON AMAZON

WHY ARE REVIEWS SO IMPORTANT?

The eBook surge has turned everything on its head. As more and more books hit the market, readers are being deluged with choices, and authors are struggling to get their books noticed.

With literally thousands of books published daily, what's an aspiring publisher or author to do? If you want to be head and shoulders above the rest and make sure your book is *discovered*, it's time to get serious about being seen where your reader will find you.

It's time to learn more about the two things most important to your reader: reviews and engagement.

Why do reviews matter? First, people like what other people like. Second, reader engagement—establishing relationships with your readers through things like reviews, giveaways, blog posts, newsletters, and so on—drives book exposure and sales. As discussed in the prior section, Amazon reviews kick-start your page's algorithm, in turn boosting your book page visibility.

In this section you're going to learn how to get more reviews, more readers, and more book sales. And it's a lot easier than you think. Marketing people love to complicate the heck out of everything. Well, not all marketing people, but many. And let's face it, there's a whole lot of confusing and conflicting information out there.

But let me make you a promise as a person who's been marketing for many, many years. The things you'll learn in this book work. I *guarantee* they do. If the methods in this book don't get you more reviews, more exposure, and more sales, return it to me personally for a full refund.

GETTING PROFESSIONAL REVIEWS

Everywhere you turn you hear stories about the "shrinking review window." It's tougher than ever to get reviews for your book. Even though it's enough to scare off even the bravest of book marketers, it's important enough that my company has become extremely creative—and successful—at getting reviews.

One of the first things to remember is, it's not so much about who writes the review, it's about who *reads* the review. Too often authors are blinded by names like *New York Times* and *Wall Street Journal,* and they overlook publications more suited to their book.

Certainly it would be great to get a review in one of the majors, and if your book meets their guidelines, why not? But these national newspapers have thousands of books sent to them each month, and competition is fierce.

Search out publications specific to your market, and you'll increase the likelihood of getting a review. Don't waste your energy going after the wrong target. While you're pulling your review list together, dig below the surface.

Media is divided into three tiers: National, regional, and trade. Trade media is often the most overlooked segment of a campaign. But there's gold in the trades, because the farther you go down in the media food chain, the hungrier the media. And that means a greater chance of being reviewed.

Once you've found an audience to target, take some time to think about your review packet. Are you dressing and stuffing it like a Thanksgiving turkey? Most reviewers don't like fancy folders or a million pieces of paper. And forget food, gifts, and other forms of bribery. They turn a reviewer off.

Instead, streamline your review packet. Include a press release, bio, contact info, a fact sheet about the book, a mock review[1], and a straightforward marketing outline—a single page with bullet points detailing your

---

1 Written by the author or book-marketing specialist. If a reviewer is pressed for time, they can tweak the mock review and include it in their publication.

marketing plans. Or include a single page with your contact information and a link to the press packet information on your author website.

Including a marketing outline shows the reviewer you're serious about the book's future. If a reviewer gets ten books in a day and can't decide which one to read first, they may pick the one with a marketing plan, because the reviewer knows their review, as well as their valuable time, won't be wasted. Plus, knowing the author is putting marketing muscle behind it is always appealing!

Part of the review packet is, of course, your book. Since there's always a chance your print book may be separated from your packet, be sure to add your contact information and vitals to the book. The best way is to list your name, publication date, publisher, and your contact information on a label and stick it on the inside cover of your book. That way the reviewer can always return the review to you.

Keep in mind that many reviewers will review only galley proofs or advance reading copies of a book. These are pages printed before the book is bound and published. For print-on-demand authors, you're out of luck unless you get galleys printed several months ahead of time.

If your target reviewer won't read digital copies and you're working from a finished book, don't despair! You can still use a finished book for reviews. Just be careful to list the publication date inside the cover jacket, on a label, so it doesn't obstruct your cover, and add a "Galley copy" label on the front cover. These don't have to be special labels; you can print them yourself. It's pretty much industry standard to do this for early reviews. And remember, if you're going after pre- and post-publication-date reviewers, you have to honor their timing requirements.

Another way to get reviews is to search for websites, blogs, or newsletters related to your topic and pitch your book to them for review. The key is to go after a reviewer and target audience with a vested interest in your topic. Pitching to trade media and online media in your specific market will help you increase your chances of being reviewed. It's better to be reviewed in a publication where 100% of the readership is your audience, than a bigger or perhaps better-known publication with 1 to 2% of your readership.

Although getting reviews from online media and traditional media is more challenging these days, it's not impossible. With the right target, a streamlined packet, and some online footwork, you can beat the statistics and get your book reviewed.

Watch campaign creativity work for you to get reviews that will help drive interest and sales to your book!

UNDERSTANDING THE REVIEW PROCESS

Over the years the review process has changed considerably. Years ago, when I first worked in the industry, there were only two types of reviews: Pre- and post-publication-date reviews. The publication date was essentially your book's "birthday"—the day it was launched, also called a "street date," or "in-store" date if you were lucky enough to get into bookstores.

You still have the same two types today, but the market has changed. *How* you utilize each of them will make all the difference in getting your book noticed.

When a book is published traditionally, the publisher determines the publication date. That date is often a year out, because traditional publishers must plan that far in advance. Things just move slowly in that world.

If you've self-published, are going to self-publish, or own your own publishing company, you can determine the date. Be sure to leave yourself at least a three- to four-month window for reviews and blurbs and testimonials—pre-publication reviews. While you're navigating through various reviewers' information, you'll see from their submission guidelines how much of a window they want.

PRE-PUBLICATION VERSUS POST-PUBLICATION REVIEWS

Reviews are still divided into these two categories, and although you can go after prepublication reviews, you want to aim for post-publication reviews. These reviews happen anywhere from the day your book is "born" to weeks or months after.

Post-publication is where you're golden. While pre-publication reviews are great, major publishers own a lot of this landscape. With all the big publishers put out there, the field for pre-pub reviews is crowded. Post-pub is a different story. This doesn't mean you shouldn't pursue pre-pub reviews, just put more effort into what's really going to pay off.

With post-pub reviews, as long as you continue to find new reviewers who will accept your book, push it as hard as you can for as long as you can. I continue to pitch most of my books months after their publication dates. It's well worth the effort. Remember, it's about discovery. People like what other people like. The more people you get talking about your book, the more people will go looking for it.

ADVANCE READING COPIES (ARCS) OR GALLEYS

In pitching to pre-pub reviewers, you should know some of the ins and outs of the trade. If you're going to push for early reviews, you'll need to get copies of your book printed for mailing. Advance reading copies of a book are called ARCs or galleys.

ARCs don't have to be perfect. Most advance reading copies include a statement on the cover that says, "Advance Reading Copy, not for resale," and reviewers know it may still have typos and perhaps not even a final cover.

If your book is 80% ready, meaning you've finished the major edits but have one final proofing pass to go, you can get this draft bound and sent to reviewers who require an actual print book. Your local copy shop can do a tape binding, which is easier to ship than a spiral-bound book. Also, printing off a neatly prepared Word doc is fine.

The book doesn't have to be typeset, though I've done it both ways. Ideally, you'll send a final or near-final cover with the book. If you don't have one yet, at the very least send a mock-up.

People often make the process of creating an ARC more complicated than it needs to be. Remember that, while presentation is important, it's about the book itself. From a reviewer's perspective, that's how you'll be judged.

If you go with a galley or an ARC, include a sheet similar to the one on the next page. Just insert it at the front of the book. For nonfiction, you'll want to provide a brief description of the book and a clear outline of its benefits. For fiction, just the description is fine. Be sure to include any early endorsements you've gotten for the book, too.

Most bloggers post their blog policies and genre preferences—it's important to read their policies in order to understand how far in advance they may need to review your book. If you're working on a tight time frame and they indicate it could take six months to get to your book, you might not want to pitch to them. Then again, if your book is in a small niche, and this blogger and site seem perfect for you, a longer wait might be worth it.

SAMPLE ARC INFORMATION SHEET

ADVANCE READING COPY—NOT FOR RESALE

From Book to Best Seller

An Insider's Guide to Publicizing and Marketing Your Book

YOUR ROADMAP TO BECOMING A BEST-SELLING AUTHOR.

Congratulations—you're published! Whether you're promoting your first book or your fiftieth, *From Book to Best Seller* will help transform your marketing campaign from ordinary to extraordinary. *From Book to Best Seller* is your step-by-step guide to success. You'll learn how to plan and launch a super-savvy book marketing program without breaking a sweat.

Here's what's inside:

- A step-by-step guide to developing the perfect publicity plan for your book
- How to get on radio and TV—today!
- Planning a super-successful book signing
- The secrets to crafting an exceptional press kit
- How to sell thousands of books through specialty retailers
- How to get your book into book clubs
- How to launch a successful publicity campaign on the Internet

ISBN: 1600370896 Paperback
Page Count: 250 pages
Genre: Nonfiction – Marketing
Pub Date: Spring 2019
Price: $9.95 eBook - $18.95 Paperback – $39.95 Audio
Format: Paperback – eBook – Audio
Trim: 6 x 9
Page Count: 296

MARKETING AND PUBLICITY INFORMATION:

Extensive Internet promotion, including a Virtual Author Tour™, advance launch planned for *From Book to Bestseller* with top fifty book reviewers in print media, promotional push into publishing media (print and broadcast), book-club submission, book-review campaign, freelance article submission, and announcement to author's mailing list of five thousand.

Speaking engagements already booked for 2020.

ABOUT THE AUTHOR

Penny is a book marketing and media relations specialist. She coaches authors on their projects, manuscripts, and marketing plans, and teaches a variety of courses about publishing and promotion. Her company, Author Marketing Experts, Inc., specializes in nontraditional promotion for exceptional results. You can visit her website at www.amarketingexpert.com.

MUST-DOS BEFORE PITCHING TO REVIEWERS

No matter how compelling your book and pitch, you can only go so far if you haven't taken care of the basics.

And nothing is more basic than a website. You have one, right?

You should, and your site should be easy to read and navigate. You don't need fancy graphics or inspiring music: A clean, professional design and easy-to-find features are all you need. Your home page should include your book cover, book synopsis, a buy-this-book-now button, and links to interior pages on your site where visitors can learn more.

These interior pages should include an author's page with a bio. You may include a longer bio, but have a short version—about 250 words—ready to use for reviews, press releases, and pitches. Also, have a nice downloadable photo reviewers or media can use. The photo should be in focus. You may say, "Duh," but we've seen plenty of author websites with blurry photos. The photo should be professional, without a lot of clutter in the background. You should also have a high-quality, downloadable book cover photo or graphic image (.jpeg, for example) available. Some of the other pages and items you'll want to include are outlined below:

- A page for reviews, blurbs, and testimonials, updated as soon as you have new material.
- A book excerpt may not be required, but it's highly recommended. Given how competitive review space is, this is something that can make the difference between a review request and a polite "No, thank you." Include a link to the excerpt in your pitch and press release (PR) for the book, so it's easily accessible.
- A page with links to buy your book. List all applicable sites and

include a way for visitors to click through to them to make purchases.
- A page with contact information. If you're an expert on a timely, in-the-news topic, or want to make it easy for the media to find you, include a phone number as well as your e-mail address.
- Links to articles or blogs you've written.

The idea is to make it as easy as possible for prospective interviewers or reviewers to learn all about you and your book.

Bells and whistles can't disguise a weak website. Ensuring that the basics are there so visitors can easily learn all about you and your book (and review it or buy it) is critical. Visitors only spend seconds visiting websites; if they don't see what they need or want, they move on.

Make your site inviting and informative so they'll stick around and explore.

BLOG TOURS: HOW TO GET MORE BLOG REVIEWS FOR YOUR BOOK

In addition to pitching to reviewers, consider pitching to bloggers, too—it's a great way to get publicity, and to find more reviewers.

It's important to understand the differences between these two ways to harvest reviews. While pitching to reviewers can lead to coverage at any time, unless you've worked out a time frame with the reviewer, a blog tour typically covers your book for a specified time frame by a specified number of bloggers. On a blog tour, an author goes from blog to blog instead of from store to store, which is what happens during a traditional book tour. Depending on the author and the blog, tours generally last a week to a month, and consist of reviews, interviews, guest posts, and giveaways.

Be sure to do your homework before jumping into a tour.

First, ensure the blog tour company you're working with has access to blogs that make sense for your book. If you've written a psychological thriller but most of their blogger contacts read romance, they're probably not the right company for you.

Second, figure out exactly what you'd like to do during your tour. For example, you may not want to write a lot of guest posts; many authors I know just don't have the time. If you're short of time, you'll want to limit your availability or offer book excerpts instead. In most cases, however, especially if you make yourself available for interviews or guest blog posts, most bloggers will give you plenty of time.

Third, figure out how long you'd like the tour to last so you know how many bloggers you'll need. Keep in mind, though, that you might end up being at the mercy of a very busy blogger schedule. A good rule of thumb is to have guest posts ready to go beforehand, then do your research to uncover the best prospects to pitch to. Some bloggers love blog tours; others don't. Just give yourself plenty of time to set up your tour. Bloggers are busy, and will sometimes decline due to other commitments, so you'll want to have alternatives in place.

As you set up your tour, you'll want to get each blogger's name, contact information, and preferred genres. If your genre is a natural fit for them, you can use that in your pitch. Also, become familiar with their style.

Some bloggers emphasize only the positive, and if they can't say anything nice they may decline to review the book. Others prefer to be honest, sometimes brutally, but most bloggers will reach out to the author and give them the option of not posting a negative review. Bloggers know how tough it is out there and will rarely slam a book unless there's something hideously wrong with it.

As you peruse the blogs you're targeting, get a sense of their tone *before* approaching them. And honestly ask yourself how you'd feel having your book reviewed in that tone. If you can't handle it, don't pitch to that blogger. There are hundreds of blogs to pitch to, so be choosy.

And trust your instincts. You may find a gem of a blog with a low Google page rank, but if it's a nice-looking site, the posts are well written, it has regular commenters, and basically demonstrates a commitment to reviewing books, make a pitch! Once you find blogs you like, look at their blogrolls for additional blogs to check out—often bloggers who like similar books list each other's websites.

CRAFTING THE PERFECT BOOK REVIEW PITCH

Once you've built a list of potential reviewers, it's time to start pitching.

While this may not be as difficult as achieving world peace, it's amazing how many authors make serious mistakes at this stage. You simply can't afford to do that.

With thousands of books being published every day, competition for reviews is fierce. The average new book, if not heavily promoted by one of the major New York publishing houses, is not likely to get much in the way of newspaper or magazine reviews. That kind of review space has been shrinking for years.

Meanwhile, there has been considerable growth in book blogging and online reviewing. Although even with this growth, far more books are being published than there are bloggers available to review them. Understand that most reviewers do this as a labor of love and make little or no money. Their review blogs are not full-time endeavors, but something they work into often already-busy lives. Learning how to make a great first impression with your pitch is crucial.

Fiction and nonfiction authors often use different approaches when pitching.

For fiction, seek bloggers who review books in your genre. If your book covers topics in which you're an expert, you may have some additional options. For instance, if you've heavily researched the history of a city or historical figure, you may find history buffs who will be open to reviewing your book. Sometimes it helps to brainstorm a list of topics from your book, fact or fiction, in order to generate ideas for what types of publications or bloggers or reviewers to target.

With nonfiction, you're an expert on the topic(s) at hand and should look for peers in those areas who can help you find reviewers. Especially since nonfiction is much more competitive, it's smart to turn competitors into allies. See if you can find ways to help them—and use that as part of your pitch. You never know what kind of partnerships you can develop if you don't ask.

Now in terms of pitching, whether in fiction or nonfiction, it makes all the difference when you're familiar with the most effective way to approach reviewers. Most bloggers identify themselves somewhere on their blogs. If they don't sign their posts, the "about me" section usually has their name. Use it! When you use a blogger's name, one thing is instantly clear: You actually took the time to find out who you're pitching to. That's a big plus.

Briefly introduce yourself. Then don't just ask them to review your book. Give them a reason, but keep it short, sweet, and to the point. Your e-mail subject line should also be brief yet clear: "Review request: Name of Book/Genre," is effective. You don't have room to write a novel on the subject line, and you want the recipient to know right away what your e-mail is about. Here's a sample of an effective pitch:

Dear Amy,

My name is Joe Smith, author of the historical fiction novel *Under the Sun*. I came across your blog and think my new title could be one that many of your readers would be interested in. *Under the Sun* is a turn-of-the-century, star-crossed lovers themed story with a heart-stopping twist! There is also a lot of great content you can learn more about at www.joesmith.com. I'd love to send you a review copy. Could you let me know your preferred format? Thank you in advance for your time!

> **Bonus!**
>
> There are more pitch samples at the end of this book.

In addition to a fantastic pitch, be sure to include the following basic book information in your e-mail:

- Title
- Author
- Genre/Niche/Subject
- ISBN (the thirteen-digit ISBN of your preferred format, hardcover or paperback)
- ASIN (if eBook only)
- Publication date (month, year)
- Pages
- Price
- Publisher
- Your website link (this should also be included in your press release, which you'll send out with copies of your book, or attach to emails along with a digital ARC)

During your research phase, you'll learn things about a blogger that will help you get a review request. For instance, if they love a particular author and your book is in a similar vein, you can put that in your pitch.

If you're comfortable having a little fun with your pitch, by all means do. I once saw a pitch for a frothy romance that asked potential reviewers if they'd like to sin with a duke—very catchy and appropriate for the book.

But don't force it. If it's not your style, don't worry about it. It's far more important to explain who you are, what your book is about, and why this reviewer would be interested in your book. Provide links to your website so they can learn more about you and your book and request a review copy. And when they follow up by clicking on your links, make sure whatever information they'll need is in place and easily accessible.

You may or may not hear back right away. Some bloggers check their e-mail daily, others weekly. Be patient. It's fine to follow up in a couple of weeks if you feel you matched up well with a particular blog and haven't heard back. It's always possible that your original e-mail ended up in spam or was overlooked. The sheer volume of review requests reviewers receive is often staggering.

After that, if there's still no word, move on. Seek reviews from other bloggers.

TURNING YOUR BOOK INTO
A 24/7 SALES TOOL

Let your book go to work for you. You can use the book itself to encourage reviews.

One of our clients, a first-time, unknown author, was ready to market her book. We knew that, given her genre—contemporary romance—the potential for receiving reviews was low. We decided to encourage reviews by having her write a request letter to her readers at the end of her book. In her letter, she politely asked for feedback and a review. She now has nearly 70 reviews on Amazon. Simple but effective!

And remember, she was a first-time author with no online history—and she self-published. Even with all these things working against her, she got tons of reviews. Were they all five-star? No, but let's face it, a book page populated with tons of five-star reviews is often considered suspect anyway. All her reviews were authentic, written by real readers the author became engaged with. What's more, those readers are now part of her "tribe." She stays in touch with them and lets them know whenever another one of her books comes out.

For her second book, we encouraged her to actually write a letter explaining how tough it can be to get reviews and encouraging her readers to review her book(s) on Amazon and Goodreads. She also thanked them for buying her book. The result was amazing. Here's the letter, if you'd like to try it out for yourself. Do note that the style of the letter should be revised for whether you're a fiction or nonfiction author. Feel free to copy this or revise it—whatever you feel works for you—but use it. It works!

Thank you for reading!

Dear Reader,

I hope you enjoyed *Shelf Life: The Publicist,* book 2. I have to tell you, I really love the characters Mac and Kate. Many readers wrote me asking, "What's next for Nick?" Well, be sure to stay tuned, because the saga of publishing drama isn't quite over. Nick will be back in book 3. Will he find his happy ending? I sure hope so.

When I wrote *The Publicist,* book 1, I got many letters from fans thanking me for the book. Some had opinions about Mac and Kate, while others rooted for Nick. As an author, I love feedback. Candidly, you're the reason I will explore Nick's future. So tell me what you liked, what you loved, even what you hated. I'd love to hear from you. You can write me at authorchristinageorge@gmail.com and visit me on the web at www.thepublicistnovel.com.

Finally, I need to ask a favor. If you're so inclined, I'd love it if you would post a review of *Shelf Life.* Loved it, hated it—I'd just like to hear your feedback. Reviews can be tough to come by these days, and you, the reader, have the power to make or break a book. If you have the time, here's a link to my author page, along with all my books on Amazon: www.amzn.to/19p3dNx

Thank you so much for reading *Shelf Life* and for spending time with me.

In gratitude,

Christina George

Just a few things about this letter.
First, you can't ask for just good reviews.
Second, a lot of people may read this as an eBook, so be sure to put

a live link in the book, preferably a link to your Amazon Author Central page. When you're putting your book together, you won't have the actual link to the Amazon page it's on. And of course you want your readers to see all your books, not just the one they're reading.

And be sure to add this letter to the last page of your book, not the front matter. A lot of authors like to write letters to their readers, but that's not the purpose here. You want to thank them for reading a book they just finished. If your request is at the front, they'll forget about it by the time they get to the end.

THE BENEFITS OF CROSS-PROMOTION

Another way to engage readers is to attract them from one book to the next. Generally, when you are reading a book on Kindle and you get to the end of the book, it will send you over to the book's page and ask you to rate it. One thing the Kindle device doesn't do is send readers to the author's Amazon page, where they can find out about the author's other books. Kindle's in the business of selling books, so referring you to the Also Bought section makes more sense for them, but it's not true for you. Cross-promoting your books is an invaluable sales strategy.

OTHER WAYS YOU CAN CROSS-PROMOTE YOUR BOOKS

- List your other titles with excerpts at the back of your book. If you have too many, pick two or three, and vary which ones you mention in each of your books, meaning that in book X you reference titles A and B, and in book Y you mention books C and D.
- Include a book excerpt or excerpts with the book mentions.
- Create a special offer that links to your website or, ideally, takes them to a special page on your website that takes your reader to your special offer. Maybe as a thank-you give them a free download of one of your books or special reports. In exchange for this freebie, you get their e-mail address. This does two things: First, the freebie builds goodwill with your reader, and second, you're collecting their e-mail for future promotions.

BONUS TIP:

Get a URL that best describes your niche. For me, it's www.SellMoreBooksonAmazon.com. This URL has (in the past) forwarded to my Amazon author page. Now it goes to our Amazon program.

HOW TO FIND SOCIAL MEDIA INFLUENCERS

Social media influencers can provide you with nearly priceless credibility and reviews because they're already tapped into their markets, and they've quite literally created a brand around people trusting snippets of their opinions.

Finding social media influencers to pitch for a review takes some targeted research, but it's much more straightforward than you might think.

The one thing to keep in mind is, you likely don't want to go after the influencers with millions and millions of followers, because, if we're being honest, big name brands are sending them free swag and pitching them for reviews and features. So aim to find influencers who have several hundred or even several thousand followers, and start there.

It definitely works in your favor if you're already on the platform you're pitching to, because you'll need to send your personalized message from the platform itself, and anyone you reach out to for a review will check to see if you're following them. That's just the reality.

You can find influencers by searching categories and hashtags. Instagram, for example, will be both because they provide both, but Twitter would predominantly be hashtags. Facebook doesn't have influencers like Instagram and Twitter do, so we won't go there.

Once you find the individuals who seem to be leading the charge for topics that are directly related to your book, start sending them private messages, use your elevator pitch, and offer them a free copy of the book for review.

If you're looking for book influencers specifically, you can search for #bookstagram on Instagram and check out who's helping book lovers live their best life!

So if you're on Instagram or Twitter, and want to aim for some influencer reviews, start doing some research, follow the people who seem like your best bet, snoop around to ensure you understand what they typically like and don't like, and what they feature often, get to know their personality a bit, comment, and like some of their posts—and when you're ready, offer them a copy of your book.

THE SECRET TO DOUBLING THE NUMBER OF REVIEWS YOU RECEIVE

Last year I conducted an experiment to see if I could double or triple the reviews I could get if I was an unknown, newly published author. If you've ever tried to get reviews, you know it's tough for a first-time author. You're lucky to get one or two at most.

I always tell authors to personalize their pitches. Most of the time they just sort of nod vaguely. But I suspect few actually do it, because it can be time-intensive. Not only do you have to go to the reviewer's blog, find their name, look up some of the books they've reviewed, decide if they're right for your book, and then pitch to them—but to ensure your success, you need to take it a step further. Find and include some personal information about your reviewer too.

For example, I was pitching to a reviewer and noticed that she had a dog named Library, so I included it in my pitch. It personalizes your communication, and shows you're paying attention and chose to approach them specifically, which is important! Whenever I did this, I tripled and even quadrupled the number of review requests I got for this unknown author.

Personalizing each e-mail may seem tedious and time-consuming, but sending out hundreds of e-mails that receive no response, not getting reviews for your book, and therefore selling less, are infinitely worse. All this initial legwork paves the path for future success in this market.

And if you keep a list of these e-mail contacts in an Excel document, when you publish to this market again, your one-time effort will be maximized. You won't have to redo the research because you can pull from the list you already have.

Relationships take time, but you'll find that if you've already built them for the first book, getting reviews for the second takes half the time.

HOW TO RESPOND TO A REVIEW

Most of the time when we get reviews, they're good. Sometimes they're even great. Occasionally, though, you may get a review that's not so great.

Unfortunately, not everyone will love your book. When that happens, just let it go. But before you do, thank the reviewer anyway for reading your book. They may ask you if you still want them to run the review. The choice is yours, of course, but unless it's truly bad and meant to be hurtful, every review deserves at least a response.

HOW TO RESPOND TO REVIEWS USING AUTHOR CENTRAL

When you log onto your Author Central account, look for the blue bar at the top. You'll see a button for customer reviews.

This button will take you to the page shown below, where you'll see a bunch of your reviews. Under each review you'll see the, "Add a comment," button, where you can respond to reviews. It's a great way to connect with your readers on Amazon!

Here's a screenshot:

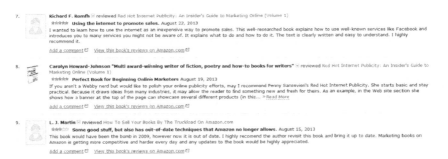

REVIEW INCENTIVES

If you have a gift that ties into your product—swag—it's totally fine to send it to the reviewer. Seriously. Reviewers *love* swag, as long as it's classy and not junk.

Incentives can be a great way to pull in reviewers, so send swag with your book. We offered a book-themed tote bag for the first 25 reviews on one book and ended up getting almost all 25 reviews overnight because fans were so eager for the tote bag.

And get creative. There are lots of charming, fun, and often useful things, such as the tote bag mentioned above, which can promote a book's location or theme or represent a protagonist's personality. You can find useful things that are often associated with your topic. A couple more examples include a novel set in Belgium that was accompanied by a small box of Belgian chocolates, and a motivational title sent with practical pocket journals.

Just make sure you tell your reviewers you want an honest review, good or bad.

And keep it on the up-and-up—unlike the guy who was so desperate to get reviews he offered an all-expenses-paid cruise for the best review but had no intention of actually providing the cruise. While this wasn't illegal, it was unethical. The author got a lot of reviews, but he also had several people post reviews on his Amazon page calling out his scam. Not a smart approach in the end.

One of the best incentives you can offer your reviewers is to express sincere gratitude. Always, always, always send a thank-you, either with the book or after. Even if you don't like the review, thank them anyway. You'll cast your net even wider if you do. Reviewers talk. Be grateful, no matter what. They'll genuinely appreciate that.

GIFTING EBOOKS

Gifting eBooks is fun way to use the Amazon.com system. You can gift eBooks to reviewers who request a MOBI (Kindle-formatted) copy of the book, or you can gift them to various readers to help generate buzz and drive sales.

Be sure to drop the price of the book before gifting, though, because the gifting process will cost you less if you do. I generally drop the price of my book to $0.99 before gifting. And while it'd be nice to gift your book during your freebie giveaway time, Amazon won't let you. The book has to be at a certain price point—whatever pricing you determine.

Gifting a book does not necessarily mean everyone will actually download it, because they can use the price of the book to buy something else. Which is why I keep the pricing low—so it's too much work to flip it into something else and much more appealing to download your book.

When you gift the book, Amazon will send you to a form you can fill out with any message you want to include. Just complete the form and hit "Send."

You will be charged per book you send, but you will *not* be paid royalties until the recipient downloads it. That means if they don't see the e-mail notification—if it winds up in spam or whatever—you'll still be charged but won't get your cut. You can circumvent this problem by sending the book to people you actually know. That way they'll be more inclined to download it. Also, be sure to send them an e-mail in advance to let them know it's coming, so if it doesn't show up in their inbox they can check spam.

Gifting eBooks can help spike sales statistics, especially if everyone is downloading the book on the same day. And, as a final tip, if you want to spike your book in a particular category, encourage your friends or followers to download immediately so it'll have a greater impact on your Amazon presence!

HARNESSING THE POWER
OF GOODREADS

Goodreads is a front-and-center social network for authors—even more so since Amazon purchased Goodreads in 2013, and they're now topping out at more than 85 million global users.

Although many authors and publishers vowed to close their Goodreads accounts after the merger, it seems Goodreads is still going strong and maintaining its independence. Goodreads CEO Otis Chandler cites three primary factors behind this acceleration: "A critical mass of book reviews," "explosive" mobile growth, and international expansion.

If you're not on Goodreads, or if you haven't touched your account in a while, you should consider the benefits this site offers.

There are many success stories about authors who "got noticed" there after mingling with other members and ultimately getting tons of reviews. While success isn't guaranteed, Goodreads can help you get a leg up on your promotion.

To know what does and doesn't work on Goodreads, it helps to understand the average demographic of the site: adult females, well-educated, higher incomes, mothers, and predominantly Caucasian and Asian.

As an author, your number-one goal on Goodreads should be to get reviews. Some of the most successful authors and books that were once "dark horses" came up in the ranks through the power of Goodreads in terms of both reader engagement and reviews.

Goodreads reviews work harder than most reviews because they're syndicated to USAToday.com, e-commerce sites, and library-related sites.

One note about Goodreads reviews: Reviewers and readers sometimes go to war on Goodreads. If someone doesn't like your book, let it go. It's a much trickier walk if you start to fight a reviewer who has a huge following battling right along with her. Stay positive. Not everyone will like your book, even on Goodreads, but the potential for publicity is worth the risk. And a lot of times what one person didn't like could end up being exactly what another is looking for, so don't get too focused on single reviews unless you have an issue with your editing or some other cardinal publishing sin... because, well, it's time to get that fixed, and you should have caught it before you started your book promotion journey.

HERE ARE A FEW TIPS FOR GETTING MORE REVIEWS ON GOODREADS:

- Post a preview of your book on your page.
- Create a blog post that says your book is available for review.
- Use groups to get reviewed on Goodreads, but do it wisely and carefully. With many groups, you need to be an active participant or your request for reviews could create resentment. I'll talk more about this later.
- Make sure your website has a Goodreads widget. When you sign up for your account, you'll see where and how to get these widgets. It's a great way to attract an additional following.
- Schedule a Goodreads giveaway.
- Shelve, rate, and review other books
- Grow your network in thoughtful ways, such as using personal messages when asking to connect with someone and point out that you both love a certain author or genre, and make it meaningful

GOODREADS ADVERTISING

Goodreads ads have an advantage over other platforms such as Google and Facebook, because you have a captive reader audience. This is a major plus. Also, they're relatively easy to set up, and Goodreads is one of the most helpful social platforms out there. Seriously, their FAQs are truly stellar. You can read more about setting up ads here (www.goodreads.com/help/list/advertisers).

But the one drawback is that their click-through rate is low, and they admit this. That means there's not a lot of activity on the ads themselves compared to a lot of other platforms. But again, you're already working with a very targeted audience—so keep that in mind. With Goodreads, it's more of a quality over quantity thing.

Another key benefit is that for as little as $10 you can collect extremely helpful data from the clicks you do get. You can access the kinds of readers who are interested in your book, which is worth its weight in gold!

GOODREADS LISTOPIA

Goodreads Listopia is so well-organized that readers actually go back again and again, something you don't see with any other site. Essentially, Goodreads allows readers to create lists of recommended books by topic and genre—sometimes specific ones, too, like "The Best Time Travel Romance Novels."

What's the best part? You can add your own books to these lists and petition your fan base to vote on them. The more votes you have, the more exposure you get to the 50 million+ readers on the site who browse these lists for their next great book recommendations.

As with any self-promotion, keep it classy. Don't throw your books on all the lists at once. It's also a good idea to vote on other books and participate in other ways. Goodreads richly rewards authors who actually get involved and use the site the way it was intended to be used by booklovers.

And if you happen to have a network of author friends and colleagues who write in the same genre, start your own list, give it a catchy name, put everyone's books in it, and then harness the power of multiple networks when it comes to petitioning fans for votes and exposure!

GOODREADS NEWSLETTERS

Goodreads offers a few newsletters to help you stay in touch with the community, what's trending, and more.

The first is the Goodreads author-focused blog called *Authors & Advertising Blog*. This fantastic newsletter, although not published on regular schedule (or as often as their main newsletter), often has great marketing tips, ideas for promotion on Goodreads, and website shortcuts.

It's worth signing up: www.goodreads.com/author/newsletter. Their regular monthly newsletter can be found here: www.goodreads.com/newsletter. A lot of advertising opportunities are found within this newsletter. Although their webpage advertising does fairly well, I have no current data on how well the ads in their newsletters perform. If you decide to advertise in the newsletters, proceed with caution.

YOUR GOODREADS PROFILE

When you first start with Goodreads, you'll be a "user."

Once you have a user profile, you can upgrade to an author profile. There are a lot of articles out there about how to create a great profile on Goodreads. Just be sure to include a professional headshot. And don't leave any of the areas on your profile blank; fill in the "about you" section, "books you like to read" section, and so on.

Here's a quick link to the author profile info on Goodreads: www.goodreads.com/author/program.

Adding your blog to your profile is a fantastic way to promote yourself on the page. Your readers will get to know you if you consistently post good content. Also, it's a good bit of "SEO juice" with your followers, because a blog post on Goodreads generates a link, and hopefully traffic, back to your website. Simply add your blog feed by clicking on the drop-down arrow, then "edit profile" next to your picture (at the top right-hand side of the page).

If you have a book video or author video, be sure to promote it on Goodreads. It's easy to add video once you're in the profile settings. Keep in mind, it's best to pull the video directly from YouTube. Upload it there if you haven't already, instead of linking from your website. In most cases, website hosting services will charge mega fees to host videos if you're trying to host videos on your site.

Finally, it's always a good idea to have a YouTube account, because video is an important social media tool.

GOODREADS GROUPS

Groups can be great places to network, and Goodreads has thousands of groups. Some will even let you request book reviews. Try to join at least one or two right off the bat. You can add more later, when you're used to navigating the system.

To sign up for groups, simply start searching for them. In deciding on the right group, consider a few things, like genre and how active the group is. And look for a group that's robust and active so you don't waste your time.

Additionally, you can jump ship. If you find a group's activity isn't right for you, join another group or groups. You can always sign up for the original group again later. As far as I've been able to tell, Goodreads does not limit the number of groups you can join, but it's smart to join only those you can actually participate in. Otherwise, it's like showing up for a fabulous party and watching from the sidewalk. It won't do you much good, and it can get pretty cold out there.

When you join a group, it's important to remember that *first and foremost, you are a reader, not a promoter.*

While you're there to publicize your book, launching into self-promotion right off the bat is not recommended—and it could get you banned from some exceptional groups if you're not careful. Your goal is to be "helpful," so contribute to at least one discussion, preferably more. Engage first, promote later.

- If the group has freebie days (days when you can announce your Goodreads giveaway), take advantage of them. If not, don't announce your giveaway. If you aren't sure, ask the group moderator(s).
- Most groups have a bookshelf. If you want your book placed on this shelf, ask the moderator. Although, here again, it's wise to become a contributing member before you put your book on the shelf.
- Participate in things like polls and roundtable discussions. The key to being noticed in these groups is discussion. If you're not participating, you're just sitting on the sidelines watching everyone else.

Finally, you can also create your own group. It's called the "Featured Author Group," open only to Goodreads authors. Readers can discuss your book, its topics, your writing, and anything related to your book. It's a fantastic vehicle for sharing with your readers, getting to know them, and growing your base.

To start your own group, go here: www.goodreads.com/author/featured_groups.

A couple of fantastic Goodreads groups to join are listed below. Both allow you to highlight your book and request reviews.

www.goodreads.com/group/show/60696-making-connections
www.goodreads.com/group/show/26989-goodreads-authors-readers

A QUICK AND SIMPLE ACTION LIST FOR GOODREADS

In order to build your presence on Goodreads, you need to be active. This doesn't mean you need to be on the site daily. If you can, great, but if not, that's fine too. But show up in some form at least once a week:

- Add a new book to your shelves—one you're reading, one you want to read, or a book that inspired your writing.
- Customize your shelves as much as possible. This personal touch stands out.
- Write a review of someone else's book. If you do a lot of Amazon reviews, you can simply repost the content to Goodreads. And to make yourself the real "darling" of the review world, grab your Goodreads review and cross-post it to Amazon. Wouldn't you love it if someone did that for you?
- Rate books. It's easy. You don't even have to write a review; just give stars.
- Blog. If you have a blog on your website, that's fantastic, just link it. If you don't, at least update your Goodreads status once a week. It doesn't have to be a long post. You can just add a favorite book passage or an author quote. Ramp up your status updates as you near a new book release. Remember, you're aiming for profile activity.
- Post to a group, make a comment, or respond to someone's question. Being a superfan of your genre is a great way to organically build

your network of genre readers. If they start seeing your name popping up in their groups, they'll know you're the real deal and start following you. Now THAT is quality over quantity.

- Add friends at least weekly. You'll find people in groups that you want to friend or reviews you want to follow. Building a healthy friend list is key to expanding your network and getting more reviews on Goodreads. Again, just be sure to include a short but friendly personal message about why you're adding them.

- Stay current with who the top users are in your key groups. Connect with them, offer them a book for review, and don't spam. Be engaged.

THE POWER OF GOODREADS GIVEAWAYS

One of the best ways to kick-start book discovery is with a Goodreads giveaway. I recommend doing multiple giveaways for a book, and even pre-publication giveaways will help spike success and reviews on the site.

While most folks recommend long giveaways (e.g., thirty days), I recommend you run them for shorter periods. A week to ten days is optimal, because your giveaway drops off the new-giveaways list quickly, but it's also put on a list of those ending soon. If you do a shorter giveaway, you'll likely be on the "ending soon" list. The "ending soon" list covers giveaways ending in 24 to 48 hours. Be sure to post an update about this on your Goodreads page and on your blog, especially if your blog is connected to your Goodreads page.

How many books should you give away? For print I've done anywhere from ten to fifty, but it's best to keep it lower. Ten is manageable; fifty becomes unruly. While a higher number sounds great, at some point you will have to mail out print books to the winners or ship them from Amazon, and Goodreads only allows printed book giveaways at this time. If you're a KDP author and doing a Kindle giveaway, you're not paying for the books themselves, so I say go for the full 100. Why? Because that's 100 readers who now have access to your book. And your book automatically gets added to their to-read shelf, and—this is the best part—Goodreads will email winners as a follow-up to your giveaway to remind them to rate and review. It's pretty fantastic.

If you're a member of a few groups, there's likely a thread to promote giveaways in at least one of them. Find that thread and post to it. Regardless of your giveaway time frame, post it once at the beginning and again when you're nearing the end. I'm not a fan of blasting groups with "all about me" posts, so twice is my limit. You may find groups who encourage more frequent giveaway reminders, but I doubt it. Other authors on the site are trying to get attention too.

You can even use your older books for giveaways. There aren't any Goodreads rules against it. If you have a great book and are just discovering this site, do a giveaway and see what happens—especially if it's not your only book and you're writing new material. Some authors with multiple titles start with their oldest books and work their way forward.

Ready to sign up for your own giveaway? Then head over here: www.goodreads.com/giveaway.

Once there, be ready to list the start and end dates, as well as all pertinent book information, such as ISBN or AISN, book description, publisher, and number of copies you're willing to give away. Then you're ready to go with your first Goodreads giveaway!

CREATE EVENTS FOR YOUR GIVEAWAY

Use the Events feature on your profile to create an event for your giveaway. It's super simple, and a fantastic way to spread the word to your network. Plus they can invite other people to the event as a way to get more people over to your giveaway page.

As a bonus tip, use the Events feature for anything worthwhile you have to share, including discount eBook promotions, cover reveals…get creative! And use this free feature as motivation to continually grow your network!

ADVERTISING YOUR GIVEAWAY

Another way to boost exposure is to run an ad to help boost your giveaway. Ads are simple on Goodreads. They operate on a pay-per-click system, which means you only pay when someone clicks on your ad. You also buy credit, and I suggest starting at $10.00. You can always add more, but you may never use $100.00.

Get started here: www.goodreads.com/advertisers.

Goodreads openly admits that new ads generating a lot of clicks in the first few days will be shown more frequently throughout the day. Essentially,

Goodreads gives its users what they want by responding to click numbers. Make your ad content compelling, and don't go the super-cheap route when it comes to bidding on your per-click cost. The minimum is $0.10, the recommendation is usually $0.50. Some say, "Go big or go home." I say, do what you're comfortable with, but remember, higher per-click ads are given priority.

For additional insights into how Goodreads ads work, go here: www.goodreads.com/help/list/advertisers/.

Try creating two ads using different tactics. One could say something like, "Enter to WIN." The other could say something like, "Get your FREE book." The words "win" and "free" are almost always guaranteed to generate a reader reaction!

In the main content of your ad, include a short, irresistible description of your book, something that makes it stand out. Then close with, "Giveaway ends [insert date]," to help encourage people to act.

The link you include with your ad should be the link to your giveaway page. To find that link, go here: www.goodreads.com/giveaway.

On the right-hand side of the page you'll see a section entitled, "Giveaways You've Created."

A few more giveaway tips:

- Let readers know if you plan to provide signed copies.
- End your giveaway on a non-popular date, like the middle of the week, *not* on a holiday.
- Again, more countries equals more exposure.
- Mail your books promptly.
- Reach out to winners with a short, respectful follow-up. Friend them and let them know you'd love their input when they're ready.

And there's a bonus! When you've finished creating your ad, you'll be given the HTML code for a giveaway widget you can add to your blog or website.

Using the power of free to help boost your book, especially on a site like Goodreads, is a great idea. It creates opportunities to connect with new readers and opens a dialogue about your book in general.

Capitalize on this opportunity. You'll be glad you did!

GIVEAWAY FOLLOW-UP FOR PRINT

When the campaign is over, the system will provide you with winners' data, including addresses.

Be sure to use the Goodreads system to notify the winners when you're shipping the book. Congratulate them, which is another great way to connect with the person on the receiving end of your book.

Not only do your notices appear on Goodreads, but a personal note of congratulations helps encourage a review from the reader. You're no longer an anonymous writer; you've connected on Goodreads and are following each other's reviews, at the very least.

Whenever I do a Goodreads giveaway, I include a short, handwritten note when I mail the book, congratulating the person on winning and thanking them for their participation. Instead of asking for a review in the note, I encourage their feedback. I truly do want to know what the reader thinks of the book. Then I give them my e-mail address in case they want to make direct contact. A personal note is key in connecting with and engaging your readers. I also sign every one of the books I give away. Readers love signed books!

How many reviews can you actually expect? Goodreads estimates that 60% of books given away are reviewed, but I've seen numbers both higher and lower. A lot of it depends on the book, of course. Good books are reviewed more frequently. Also, it seems fiction gets a lot more reviews, but it's not a given.

GIVEAWAY FOLLOW-UP FOR KINDLE

Remember, Goodreads delivers your Kindle books for you, so the actual work on the author's part to run a giveaway is minimal. But Goodreads will also list all your winners and links to their profiles. I strongly encourage you to visit their pages, and for the readers who seem to be active on the site, congratulate them on their win and tell them you'd love to connect, and that you look forward to their rating or review because you sincerely value thoughtful feedback. The key is keeping it genuine, not spammy.

HOW TO REVIEW BOOKS

You may find this an odd chapter to include in a book about getting reviews, but posting them is important, too. Over the years I've heard from numerous folks who have friends who post reviews on Amazon, for which they are grateful, but wished they were more detailed. Many times the reviews consisted of, "Loved this book!" And while it's great to have fans, it does little to help a book sell.

When a book has lots of great, thoughtful, detailed reviews, we tend to scan them for highlights about the things that matter to us. That's how we often buy books. Both good and bad reviews can help us decide. Frankly, I've often bought a book after I read a bad review because what the reviewer didn't like was exactly what I was looking for. That's why detailed reviews are not only helpful, they're a must for your Amazon page.

It's tempting to ask friends and family to write reviews, and they often want to help but aren't sure what to say. And you may have readers who love your work but aren't savvy about posting reviews. Here are some tips you can share with those who want to post something about your book:

- Whenever possible or appropriate, ask the reviewer to add their expertise on the topic if your book relates to nonfiction.
- If you have identified your keyword strings, share them with any friends who are posting and ask them to, if appropriate, include some of them in their reviews.
- Ask readers to post reviews that are between 100 and 450 words.
- If a reader feels compelled to include a spoiler, ask them to post a warning first so the customer can choose to read on—or not.
- Never, ever, ever offer to edit a review. You want honest appraisals, not watered-down reviews that all sound alike.
- It's important that the reviewer cite why the book mattered to them.

This also personalizes the review for other readers.

If your reviewer still isn't sure how to craft a review, here are some starter questions to help them along:

1. What did you like most about the book?
2. What about the book surprised you?
3. Did the book cover the content as described?
4. Do you think you got your money's worth?
5. What could the author have done better?
6. How does it compare to other books in this category? And please mention any books you'd compare this one to.

BONUS RESOURCES

Here are some free downloads to help you get focused, get organized, and start selling more books!

Monthly Book Marketing Planner: Start filling this out to ensure you have a strategic book promotion strategy laid out in advance, saving you the stress of coming up with ideas on the fly, or missing crucial book marketing opportunities altogether.

www.amarketingexpert.com/monthly-book-marketing-planner

Quarterly Amazon Planner: Feel confident you're keeping up with all your Amazon updates and optimization strategies throughout the year.

www.amarketingexpert.com/quarterly-amazon-planner

Blog Outreach Tracker: Use this to keep track of your ongoing blogger pitching, requests, and more!

www.amarketingexpert.com/blog-outreach-tracker

Reader Profile Brainstorm: Save time, money and a lot of guesswork and missed opportunities by creating a fresh reader profile that will really help you zero in on where you need to be focusing your efforts, and the best sales angles to use for your buyer markets.

www.amarketingexpert.com/reader-profile-brainstorm

HERE ARE SOME GREAT BLOGGERS FOR YOUR PITCHES!

MYSTERY BLOGGERS

Cozy Mystery List: www.cozy-mystery.com/
Mystery Scene: www.mysteryscenemag.com
Detectives Beyond Borders: www.detectivesbeyondborders.blogspot.com/
Murder by the Book: www.mbtb-books.blogspot.com/
Murderati: www.murderati.com/

Mysteries in Paradise: www.paradise-mysteries.blogspot.com/
Mystery Fanfare: www.mysteryreadersinc.blogspot.com/
Shots: Crime & Thriller Ezine: www.shotsmag.co.uk/
Stop, You're Killing Me: www.stopyourekillingme.com/

ROMANCE BLOGGERS

Romance Reviews Today: www.romrevtoday.blogspot.com/
Magnificent: www.kbgbabbles.com/
Love Saves the World: www.lovesavestheworld.blogspot.mx
Not Another Romance Blog: www.notanotherromanceblog.blogspot.com
Penelope's Romance Reviews: www.pennyromance.com/
The Romance Reviews: www.theromancereviews.blogspot.com/

BUSINESS BLOGGERS

B2C: Business 2 Community: www.business2community.com/
Business Insider: www.businessinsider.com/
SmartBlog on Leadership: www.smartblogs.com/category/leadership/
Success: www.success.com/
Inc.: www.inc.com/
The Daily Muse: www.thedailymuse.com/
TLNT: www.tlnt.com/
Young Entrepreneur: www.youngentrepreneur.com/blog/
Under 30 CEO: www.under30ceo.com/

BOOK REVIEWERS ON THE WEB

This list includes industry standards, literary blogs, off-the-beaten-track
blogs, and the more opinion-driven book bloggers:

- **Midwest Book Review** (lists a number of sites to check out) www.
  midwestbookreview.com/links/othr_rev.htm
- **Robin Mizell:** (lots and lots of links to places that do online book
  reviews) www.robinmizell.wordpress.com/book-reviewers/.
- **Best of the Web blogs** (blog listing with a description of each blog
  listed) www.blogs.botw.org/Arts/Literature/Book_Reviews/
- **YA Book Blog Directory** (bloggers who specialize in young adult
  books) www.yabookblogdirectory.blogspot.com/p/ya-book-blogger-

list.html
- **Kidlitosphere Central** (bloggers of children's and young adult literature) www.kidlitosphere.org/bloggers/
- **FSB** (search by genre for bloggers who review those kinds of books) www.fsbmedia.com/book_blogger_search.php
- **Book Blogs Search** (a huge listing of blogs) www.fyreflybooks. wordpress.com/about/book-blogs-search/

MORE GREAT RESOURCES

- **About blog book tours**:
- www.blogbooktours.blogspot.com/2010/06/blog-tips-to-consider. html
- **Writing an effective cover letter:** www.midwestbookreview.com/ bookbiz/advice/cvr-ltr.htm
- **Writing an effective publicity release**: www.midwestbookreview. com/bookbiz/advice/prelease.htm

GET MORE READERS!

Remind people they don't need a Kindle to access eBooks. Whenever you do a book promo, mention that readers can access your book through all of these resources:
- **Kindle Cloud Reader:**
- www.read.amazon.com/about
- **iPhone and iPad apps:** www.amazon.com/gp/feature.html/ ref=kcp_iph_ln_ar?docId=1000301301
- **Android app:** www.amazon.com/gp/feature.html/ref=kcp_and_ ln_ar?docId=165849822
- **BlackBerry app:** www.amazon.com/gp/feature.html/ref=klm_ lnd_inst?docId=1000468551

PITCHING TIPS

WHEN PITCHING TO MEDIA, HERE ARE A FEW THINGS TO KEEP IN MIND WHEN SENDING LETTERS OUT:

- Always include the media person or blogger's name. If you can't find the person you're looking for, then send it to the managing editor. Usually it's easy to find a recipient's name on the company's website or by doing a simple Internet search.
- Always keep the pitch to one page.
- Always include your website URL.
- Always include a review, or partial review, if you have one from a legit source.
- Always tell them what you want—a review, feature, interview opportunity, etc.
- Always sign your letters personally.
- Always include a book if you're mailing a letter anyway.

ADDITIONAL TIPS FOR PITCHING VIA E-MAIL:

- When crafting a subject, see if their website lists special requests for how to address them. Otherwise, be straightforward, or you'll risk sounding like spam.
- Always let them know you're happy to mail them a print book or gift them one via Amazon.
- Be careful of attachments. Sometimes they get marked as spam unless you're pitching a contact who is expecting to get pitched materials. Oftentimes it's safer to list the resources, tips, etc. that you can provide upon request.

TIPS FOR FICTION:

- Always include an intriguing opening paragraph. Don't just say, "I have a book."
- When describing your story, highlight points that make your book unique.
- Leave a cliffhanger. You want them to want to find out what happens.
- Avoid copying and pasting your book description from Amazon. This is a time to take it to the next level.

SAMPLE FICTION E-MAIL SUBJECT:

"For review: New novel takes you inside the publishing industry"

TIPS FOR NONFICTION:

- Always include an intriguing opening paragraph. List the name of your book, the market it pertains to, and what makes it unique.
- Always include selling points. Lists, bullets, and other features in the book that make it better than anything else on the market are key!
- If you have a tip sheet of your own, such as a top-ten list or a single-page how-to, include that with your pitch letter. This is another opportunity to show what kind of content you're producing, and it could convince them to open your book.
- Avoid copying and pasting your book description from Amazon. This is a time to take it to the next level.
- If you're mailing letters and a copy of your book, use letterhead if your book is tied to your business.

SAMPLE NONFICTION E-MAIL SUBJECT:

"For feature: The insider's guide to marketing online"

SAMPLE LETTERS TO REQUEST REVIEWS

Date

Recipient name

Outlet or publication

Address

City, state, zip

Dear Name,

I have recently released the one marketing book every author and business owner must have in their arsenal, *Red Hot Internet Publicity: The Insider's Guide to Marketing Online.*

Authors, speakers, and small business owners have three choices these days. They can:

1. Spend a fortune on advertising and other old-school marketing techniques, and pray they'll make back their investment—against all odds.
2. Fritter away two or three years blindly stumbling around, trying on their own to figure out what works while competing for attention with more than 25 billion webpages.
3. Listen to an expert who will show them how to get their website noticed, visited, and purchased from, an expert who can show them how to be smart and successful online while keeping their dollars in their own wallet, and whose own site is in the top 1% of all the sites in the world for traffic.

"Packed with wisdom, insights, advice, and how-tos, this book should be considered your social media bible…no marketing effort is complete without it."

—Rick Frishman, Founder,
Planned Television Arts PR/
Publisher, Morgan James Books

If you would like to learn more, please visit www.amarketingexpert.com.

I appreciate your time, and hope you'll consider reviewing *Red Hot Internet Publicity*. Please don't hesitate to contact me with any questions or additional requests.

Sincerely,

Your name

Date

Recipient name

Outlet or publication

Address

City, state, zip

Dear Name,

Welcome to the world of publishing. The ego has landed.

Can one woman change an age-old institution like publishing? Probably not, but in my newly released book, *The Publicist*, Kate Mitchell sure wants to try.

As a publicist with a large, respected New York publishing house, Kate finds herself at the mercy of a broken publishing system, books that don't sell, and author egos that are often…well, as big as the island of Manhattan.

Enter the star editor, MacDermott Ellis—tall, handsome, charismatic, married, and ready to save the day. Then there's Allan Lavigne, once a revered author and now as forgotten as last year's best sellers, and his nephew Nick—tall, gorgeous, sweet, single, and ready to sweep Kate off her feet.

Kate wants to do the right thing, but her hormones seem to be driving her decisions.

As Kate tries to navigate the land-mined field of publicity, over-the-top author expectations, and the careful dance of "I'm sorry your book isn't on the best-seller list this week," she also finds authors who have been unfairly overlooked by a publisher wanting more sex, more celebrities, and more scandal.

"I've often imagined what it must be like to work in this industry…I'm sure Ms. George has more than a few industry insiders chuckling at her stories and cringing at how close to home they hit…I think The Publicist *is a nice tease of what I'm hoping will be much more to come from Ms. George."*—Scandalicious Book Reviews

If you would like to learn more, please visit www.thepublicistnovel.com.

I appreciate your time, and hope you'll consider reviewing *The Publicist*. Please don't hesitate to contact me with any questions or additional requests.

Sincerely,

Christina George

THANK YOU FOR READING!

Dear Reader,

I hope you were able to get as much out of *How to Sell Books by the Truckload on Amazon* as I intended you to.

When I wrote this book, I wanted to let you in on how to get more by the truckload: more books sold, more books reviewed. While this isn't a perfect formula, hopefully you can find ways to make it work for you.

Finally, if you have the time, I'd really love a review. Reviews are a huge help to authors, and I'm not exempt from that. Loved it, hated it—I'd just like to hear your feedback. If you have the time, here's a link to my author page, along with all my books on Amazon: amzn.to/2fg4qkK.

Wishing you much success!

Penny Sansevieri

SPECIAL OFFER!

Are you selling enough books on Amazon.com?

Now you know a lot more about promoting your book on Amazon, but there's a chance you feel a little overwhelmed as well.

So I've also designed a video series to accompany this great information, but in a visual format that walks you through a lot of these key strategies, step-by-step.

And with a one-time fee you get unlimited access to the membership platform, and it never expires, and new videos are being added all the time.

Find out more at www.amarketingexpert.com/master-amazon-video-series

**And be sure to use the code below to get
$100 off of our $199 program!**

Use this promo code: truckloadvideos

ABOUT PENNY C. SANSEVIERI & AUTHOR MARKETING EXPERTS, INC.

Penny C. Sansevieri, Founder and CEO of Author Marketing Experts, Inc., is a bestselling author and internationally recognized book marketing and media relations expert. She is an Adjunct Professor teaching Self-Publishing for NYU. She was named one of the top influencers of 2019 by New York Metropolitan Magazine.

Her company is one of the leaders in the publishing industry and has developed some of the most innovative Amazon Optimization programs as well as Social Media/Internet book marketing campaigns. She is the author of 18 books, including "How to Sell Your Books by the Truckload on Amazon," "Revise and Re-Release Your Book", "5-Minute Book Marketing," and "Red Hot Internet Publicity," which has been called the "leading guide to everything Internet."

AME has had dozens of books on top bestseller lists, including those of the New York Times, USA Today, and Wall Street Journal.

To learn more about Penny's books or her promotional services, you can visit her web site at www.amarketingexpert.com.

189